Recollections of Jacksonville

A Sesquicentennial Memoir 1872-2022

Stories of Past, Present and Future

Edited by Sam Hopkins, Jr., Ph.D.

Recollections of Jacksonville
A Sesquicentennial Memoir

Copyright 2022 by the City of Jacksonville

All rights reserved. This book may not be reprinted by any means either in whole or in parts, excluding passages for the purpose of editorial review, without the written permission of the publisher or the city maanager.

ISBN 9780980224788
Copyright
First Edition, 2022

Published by the SamPat Press
Printed in the United States of America
by Lightning Source, Inc.

Design and layout by Christine (Hopkins) Kjosa (below)
KJ Graphics

Correspondence and publication requests contact:
City of Jacksonville
315 Ragsdale
Jacksonville, Texas 75766

DEDICATIONS

Dedicated to future generations in hopes they remember the times when we have lived.

Preface

Every since I read a copy of the Jacksonville 1972 Centennial book about the city's history, prominent families, and activities, I have wanted to have someone extend that history to the sesquicentennial year of 2022. Since there was no historian available or willing to complete such a work, the solution became to ask citizens of Jacksonville to tell recollections of life that might be interesting to readers in the city's 2072 bicentennial and beyond. This book is for the descendants of the memoir writers and for all who have lived in this era. In truth, each of us should write our autobiographies for the sake of our heirs. In several instances, the memoir authors were told by members of their immediate family that they did not even know about some of the things published in the authors' stories until they read them in the newspaper. The book contains a small sampling of what life has been like in the years up to the sesquicentennial as recorded by people who have lived here. The chief sesquicentennial celebratory events, with stories and photos, are included too. These pictures are, indeed, worth a thousand words each.

The planning for the celebration of the 150th city anniversary took 18 months. The city council appointed a sesquicentennial committee to direct and manage the festivities. The committee members were Dr. Deborah Burkett, Mrs. Cassie Devillier, Mrs. Charlie Esco, Mr. Johnnie Helm, Dr. Sam Hopkins, Mr. Daniel Seguin city publicist, Mrs. Kathleen Stanfill, Mrs. Tracey Wallace, and city manager James Hubbard. The city council appropriated ample funds to support the sesquicentennial. The local businesses matched the city's help with monetary donations, material goods, and essential volunteer help. Truly, it was a community event.

Recollections of Jacksonville

The Recollections of Jacksonville publication has many contributors, starting with the people who were willing to write their memoir stories for publication in the Jacksonville Progress and the Cherokeean. One story was printed in the newspapers every week, beginning in the first week of January and continuing through to the first week of November. Michelle Dillon of the Progress and Jo Anne Embleton of the Cherokeean collaborated with Sam Hopkins, the book editor, as if he were a paper staff member. Mary Beth Scallon wrote great biographies of the very senior citizens who were the panelists in the Reminiscence Room with discussions led by Dr. Deborah Burkett. Dr. Burkett supplied information, write-ups, and photos of the events that she planned and led on Flag Day, the Dedication of a Historical Marker, and the Walk Through History. Tracey Wallace and Elizabeth Whitaker supplied valuable information and photos of the Fred Douglas High School centennial celebration. Kathleen Stanfill and Cassie Devillier planned, designed, and procured everything needed for the ever memorable, big downtown celebration on Saturday, October 22, 2022. Jacksonville added to its long history with the illustrious events that paid tribute to its magnificent sesquicentennial.

Table of Contents

SECTION 1:

Citizens' Memoirs   1

Janis Adams – Integration Memories	2-3
Mary Adamson – Healthcare in Jacksonville	4-5
Mary Adamson – Jacks 'N Jills Square Dancing	6-7
John Alexander – A Warm Loving Town	8-9
Sissy Austin – A Jacksonville Living Legend	10-11
Michael Banks – Old Main of Jacksonville Colle	12-13
Elizabeth Battle – We Are More Alike Than Different	14-15
Tamra McAnally Bolton – Visiting Downtown	16-17
Gene Brumbelow – Transplanted & Rooted	18-19
Deborah Burkett – Fabric of Jacksonville History	20-22
Al Chavira – A Hispanic's Journey	23-24
Charlie Mae Scott Esco – Humble Beginning	25-26
Mindy Folden Gellock – This is Home	27-28
Randy Gorham – Back in 1972	29
Jan Gowin – Stripling Farm and Expansion of JHS	30-31
Pat Walker Graham – A Fond Farewell	32-35
James O. Greenwood – The Livestock Market	36-38
Johnny Helm – A Good Place to Write a Song	39-40
Sam Hopkins, Jr. – It Began With Tennis	41-43
Barbara Angelo Huggins – Fondly Recalling the Past	44-45
Nathan Jones – Jacksonville, Great Place To Call Home	46-47
John Mark Lester – A Career In Education	48-49
Larry Lydick – Jacksonville, Old to New	50-52
Mike McEwen – Moving Forward, Making Strides	53-54
Jann McGaughey – Attractions Lost to Time	55-56
Bob McNiece – A Comfortable Way of Life	57
Tim McRae – The Family Auto Business	58-59

Table of Contents

Robert Nichols – Longhorns Come to Town	60-61
Charles L. Nunnally – The Pink Deal	62-63
Joe Peacock – Fifty Years Ago	64-65
Shirley Reese – A Nurse's Tale	66
Peggy Renfro – The Tomato Symbols	67-68
Hubert Robinson – We've Come A Long Way	69-70
Nancy Sonntag – My Personal Memories	71-73
Kathleen Stanfill – From Centennial to Sesquicentennial	74
Dick Stone – Jacksonville's History of Golf	75
Janice Stone – Remembering the Crosbys	76-77
Martin Swanson – Texas Basket Factory	78-79
Betty Ewalt Taylor – Rodeo Sesquicentennial Memories	80-82
Betty Ewalt Taylor – The Hometown Newspaper	82-83
John Taylor – A Child's Memory of WW-II	84-85
Judy Terry – True Blue and Gold	86-87
Harry Tilley – Coca Cola Bottling Company	88-91
Billy Jack Williams – Fred Douglas High School	92-93

Reminiscence Room Panel Stories — 94

Mary Bone Adamson MD	96-98
Shelly Shamrock Cleaver	99-101
Charles Creed DDS	102-104
Barbara Crossman	105-107
Barbara Huggins	108-110
Hallie Peoples	111-113
Sarah Robinson	114-116
Harry Tilley	117-119

Table of Contents

SECTION 2: SESQUICENTENNIAL EVENTS

Promoting a Hometown Celebration	121-124
Centennial Time Capsule Opening	125-130
Flag Day	131-134
Fred Douglas High School Centennial	135-138
Historical Marker Dedication	139-147
Walk Through History	148-153
Sequicentennial Homecoming Celebration	154-166

SECTION 1

MEMOIRS AND BIOGRAPHIES

The Sesquicentennial Committee invited some citizens in Jacksonville to write about their living experiences in our fair town. The promise to them was that their stories would be printed in the Jacksonville Progress and the Cherokeean each week from January to the first week of November. The stories would also be published in a book the Recollections of Jacksonville. The books would be family keepsakes, a legacy for future generations, and a record of 2022. The books are to be available for local purchase and by ordering on the internet at amazon.com and at BarnesandNobles.com. One copy of the book will be placed in the bicentennial time capsule. Several of the memoir authors reported that their own families said that they didn't know some of the things that had been written by the author. Those comments are a reminder that all of us should write our autobiography for the benefit of our descendants.

Integration Through the Eyes of a Child

My experience was in 1968, when the public schools were to be intergraded. I had been told stories about Fred Douglass School in Lincoln Park during my childhood from my family members. All of my family attended and graduated from Fred Douglass. My aunt and uncles told me about how beautiful the band played, how well the football and basketball team excelled, and the lovely majorettes. I was in the third grade and was anticipating attending Fred Douglass High School. The young ladies were required to wear dresses and the men were to wear dress slacks. My mother bought my clothes for the school year and of course, they were all beautiful dresses. Later that summer, I was informed by my mother that I would not be able to attend Fred Douglass because they were integrating the schools. My heart seemed like it skipped a beep or two because my dream just got shattered. I did not know the meaning of integrating, nor did I care, but I did know that I couldn't go to Fred Douglass. After crying awhile, I asked my mother what is the meaning of integrating. She explained that I would be going to the white folk's school. The blacks and the whites would be having class together.

I finally calmed down and accepted the news. I was entering the fourth grade. My friends from Elberta Elementary School were going to West Side, East Side, and Joe Wright. I lived in the vicinity of Joe Wright; so therefore, I had to attend Joe Wright. I did not know anyone in my class for the first few months, but eventually they placed some of my friends in my class. I did not have a problem with accepting the white little girls as my friends, but the problem came when I had to wear dresses everyday to school. My mother could not afford to buy me some more new clothes, so I had to wear my dresses. The children in school looked at me strangely, until finally one day one of my white friends asked me why was I wearing dresses every day? Was it because of my church status? I told her no. I explained to her that my mother had already bought my clothes because the school I thought I would be attending; the young girls could only wear dresses. She thought I was going to a catholic school. After that, no one looked at me strangely again. I never did experience any kind of racial discrimination during my time in any school. I know I was blessed.

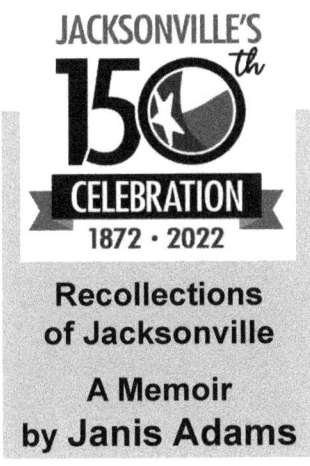

Recollections of Jacksonville

A Memoir
by Janis Adams

Healthcare in Jacksonville

There is a Facebook Group called Remember in Jacksonville When which has 4,600 individuals who have chosen to join this group to do some group remembering. Today someone posted the question, "Do you remember the Grandee Motel, initiating dozens of responses, including correction of the spelling of the Gran-Dee's name! I found a picture post card of the motel which I attached to the link – and so it goes on Facebook!

Although my family and I moved back to Jacksonville in late 1959, I did not begin working in medicine until 1963. Mrs. Otis Lake asked me to be the medical director for the new Sunset Care Center being constructed on Tena Street, which was only a few blocks from our home. The first patients I saw were in the Sunset Nursing Home which was located in a home on the west side of town. Sunset Care Center was a lovely new facility, and the experience I gained there was very valuable to me. I will always be grateful to Mrs. Lake for taking a chance on a young female physician who had been on a hiatus from the practice of medicine while my children were small.

In 1966 I began working at Travis Clinic, located in a building which had formerly been Holmes Brothers Funeral Home at the corner of S. Ragsdale and E. Larissa Streets. The clinic was at this site in 1972 when the City of Jacksonville celebrated its Centennial. Most of the women who worked at the clinic during that event dressed in attire which would have been suitable one hundred years previously. I treasure pictures taken of these employees. In 1971 the Travis Clinic Foundation purchased a 40-acre tract of land on SE Loop 456 of Jacksonville for the purpose of expansion including a new building for the clinic. A large facility was constructed and the clinic was moved there where it operated for about 10 years.

At the time of the Travis Clinic closure in 1982, multiple physicians, physician assistants, nurses and office staff were employed there. Many of the physicians, including me, continued to rent space there for another year while awaiting office space in town to become available. Some converted empty houses into offices, and others awaited office space to be constructed – such as the Professional Building adjacent to Nan Travis Hospital or elsewhere. I moved into an office on Commerce Street, which is now where Family Circle of Care is located, where I rented an office from Drs. Austin Weaver and John Storey.

After retirement 11 years later, I began working at the Cherokee County Health Department, seeing patients both in the Jacksonville clinic located in a home on Bonner Street and the Rusk office. The CCHD Jacksonville clinic remained on Bonner Street for several more years, then eventually move to the same office space I worked on Commerce Street. I retired from the CCHD after 20 years, and shortly thereafter it moved to College Avenue into a building on the former Lon Morris College campus. I continued to do volunteer work at the Mission House Clinic in Bullard until January 2020. While working there, the clinic, which was originally housed in an old home behind the First Methodist Church, moved into a new clinic on Phillip Street near the church.

So, to sum it up, every place I have worked in Cherokee County showed many changes through the years. The one place I haven't worked, but am thrilled to see it in operation is the Medical Clinic of HOPE, now housed in the remodeled building adjacent to HOPE, Inc. on Ragsdale Street. The Board of HOPE, Ellann Johnson, ED of HOPE, volunteers and, especially, Dr. Elaine Ballard and the staff of the clinic are to be commended for all they do to help those of our community who are in need.

Jacks 'n Jills Square Dancing

Square dancing in Jacksonville began after the 1972 centennial. As part of that celebration, a large event was held in the Tomato Bowl, featuring dozens of citizens dressed as those who arrived here a century earlier. Mixed in with all of those performing some action appropriate for the time, was a group of square dancers which sparked an interest in beginning a square dance club locally.

A few couples had been active in the Rambling Rose Square Dance Club in Tyler and wanted to initiate a similar club in Jacksonville. To do this, they began recruiting other couple to join with them, and especially to find a place such a club might use for lessons locally and dances for the area. Someone, I'm not sure who, contacted my husband Bob to see if we would be interested, which we certainly were. We suggested that the club meet and dance in the Fellowship Hall of the First Presbyterian Church, where we were members. Permission was obtained from the church to meet there for weekly lessons and periodic dances for area clubs to attend.

I hesitate to list early club members for fear of omitting some; but folks like Ruby and Bill Grizzard, Pat and Jay Spraggins, Jean and James Moody, Barbara and Jamie Green, and Merle and Carroll Gresham were among those early dancers. One of the first things the club did was to decide on a name. Someone suggested "Jacks 'n Jills," which was a unanimous choice as it sounded so much like Jacksonville. One of the challenges was to find someone to teach the lessons and "call" the dances. Initially, the club had various callers from the area come to instruct those just learning, and also, call for the dances. The club grew quickly and couples would bring older children. Even singles would come to learn to dance. For the first couple of years our youngest son, James, came with us, took lessons, and also learned how to square dance.

I found an article published in a copy of the Jacksonville Progress from 2010 which was written primarily to spur interest in joining the club. The article quoted Gene Sipes, one of the three remaining founding members still in the club. At that time there were 48 members in the club – the youngest was 10 and the oldest was 83 years old. The club also had a regular teacher/caller, Kenneth Melvin, city mayor (2011-2014). We had weekly lessons at the St. John's United Methodist Church. Kenneth began calling for the club many years ago while Bob and I were still active. It was awesome to have our own instructor/caller, who always did a marvelous job of both. In 2010 the club was having Fun Dances at the Norman Activity Center every second Saturday of each month with square dancers coming from all over East Texas. Square dancers do like to travel and attend not only local dances, but also district, state, and national gatherings. One of the most enjoyable square dance activities we ever attended was the National Square Dance Convention in San Antonio in 1974. Several couple from the Jacks 'n Jills attended and we all loved the "Do Sa Do By The Alamo."

Recollections of Jacksonville

Memoirs by Mary Adamson, MD

A Warm Loving, Caring Town

After accepting the position of head basketball coach at Jacksonville High School, the Alexander family moved to Jacksonville in June 1978. Moving from Post, Texas, we wondered how life would be in Jacksonville. We found a warm, loving, caring town, a town that welcomed newcomers. I still see that same town today and it must remain that way.

Being in education, one of the unique things we found about Jacksonville was it was home to two junior colleges, Lon Morris College and Jacksonville College. My favorite memory is the 1984 basketball team that made it to the state tournament in Austin. We found Jacksonville to have a unique beauty of trees, lakes, and rolling hills. With many sport organizations, we always seemed to be at some kind of game. We must make sure that we keep all kinds of organizations for young people. Jacksonville is very fortunate to have an excellent education system; and the only way we can keep it is through parent involvement in their kids' lives and education.

Tomato Fest, the Tops in Texas Rodeo, and other smaller events keep people coming to Jacksonville to visit. After moving to Jacksonville, I learned about the history of the Tomato Bowl. Everyone in East Texas knows about the Tomato Bowl., and after the remodeling the Tomato Bowl became a must for people to see. All of the things we have, the Jacksonville College, our beautiful school campuses and facilities, the many churches, the many manufacturing plants, and a growing downtown area are the result of caring people. You cannot let this die.

I was fortunate to coach and teach in a great school district for 19 years. When my wife and I retired from the JISD, many people asked us where we were moving to. We both replied nowhere, WE ARE HOME.
Outside of going to the state tournament, my greatest school memory was having cafeteria duty for my last 18 years. I was the only teacher in the in the school that saw every student everyday with lots of memories there.

Another great memory is from the first Tomato Fest or one of the first ones. Held at the Livestock Show Barn area, it features the Battle of San Tomato between city employees and school employees and teachers. The city employees were throwing the tomatoes, while the JISD were throwing also. But the JISD maintenance employees had built a couple of air powered bazookas to shoot the tomatoes: advantage JISD.

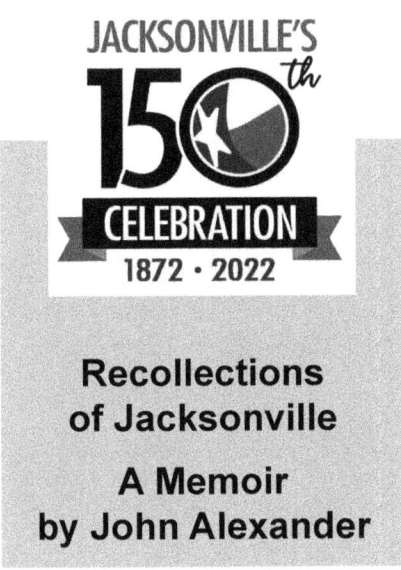

Sissy Austin, a Jacksonville Living Legend

"If at first you don't succeed, try doing it the way Sissy told you". Well said and very true, for this quote is prominent in Austin Bank and around the Austin household. Barnes Broiles, former Editor and Publisher of the Jacksonville Daily Progress, in an editorial in late 1977 concluded his remarks saying "So with 'our Sissy' as the leader, expect great accomplishments this coming year (1978) in Jacksonville". Sissy was the first woman elected to head the Jacksonville Chamber of Commerce.

She is certainly 'our Sissy', for Sissy was born Laurel Ann Phillips to Wallace "Windmill" and Annie Laurie Phillips in Jacksonville. She graduated as valedictorian of the JHS class of 1959. Sissy is probably one of the few who as a youngster could break down and repair bicycles, then progress to providing equations for the Apollo 11 moon mission in 1969. Are you surprised? Well, you must not know Sissy? Her parents were educators with Masters Degrees, so little wonder Sissy had an inquiring mind.

She earned a B.S. in Mathematics at University of Oklahoma in 1963 with outstanding grades. Sissy was most active in Campus Activities as evidenced by being recognized as a "Big Woman on Campus." She earned recognition as a Who's Who in American Colleges and Universities and from the Alpha Lambda Delta (Scholastic Sorority). Sissy was involved with tutoring at OU and was part of a research grant involving computers, with the thought of being hired by IBM or Hewlett-Packard to focus on computers.

However, during a visit to Houston, she toured NASA where she was offered a job when she helped solve an equation that had stumped the regular employees. She stated she did not know how difficult the problem was, but they just said 'I'm hung up on this. I said something like, 'Oh let me help you.' The problem was solved, a job offered and accepted without completing an application. She began working for NASA in June 1963 with the assignment to the Apollo project to develop a flight program. The Apollo project created excitement and awe while pulling the nation together. Sissy became a part of history.

Sissy is a person who believes in hard work, being prepared, achieving success, but also believes in giving back to the community while helping others to have an opportunity to succeed.

She joined Austin Bank in 1972 to begin another distinguished career.

She was instrumental in the bank developing from a small bank to the over $2.5 billion bank of today with 35 locations in East Texas. Sissy was Chief Lending Officer for many years as well as a member of the Board of Directors and Executive Committee of the bank.

She proved that she could give back to the Community for not only did she serve as President of Jacksonville Chamber of Commerce, she has served as: Regent and Board Chairman of Stephen F. Austin State University; President Cherokee Country Club; Advisory Council, Texas Tech School of Banking; Director and Chairman of Trinity Mother Frances Health Care System and served her church, First United Methodist Church as Chairman of Finance Committee and Chairman of Board of Trustees. She was Class Vice President at Southwestern Graduate School of Banking at SMU. Sissy was recognized by many organizations: Business & Professional Women as Woman of the Year; Chairman's Award from Texas Bankers Association; Jacksonville Citizen of the Year, Jacksonville Business Woman of the Year.

What a busy life, but she and husband Jeff found time to raise a family (three children and six grandkids), travel, water ski, snow ski, enjoy camping, and relaxing. Sissy knows the value of a kind word, a helping hand and mentoring, for she received them at a critical time in her life. Sissy is modest, but quietly has provided mentoring and financial aid to many over the years. She is known as a person of courage, wit and wisdom, who can be trusted.

Business and organizations have benefited from Sissy's wisdom and advice. To quote Barnes Broiles again, "With 'Our Sissy' as the leader, expect great accomplishments". NASA, Austin Bank, Trinity Mother Frances Health Care System, Stephen F. Austin University, Texas Tech School of Banking, First United Methodist Church, Pi Beta Phi can all attest to the expertise, commitment and care given by Sissy. So "If at first you don't succeed, try doing it the way Sissy told you." Many did and, thus, have experienced much success. Her family is proud of her contributions to others, but love her mostly because of whom she is at home.

JACKSONVILLE'S 150th CELEBRATION 1872 · 2022

Recollections of Jacksonville

A Memoir by the Austin Family

Old Main of Jacksonville College

A few of our historic buildings have been restored in our town of Jacksonville, Texas, but most have been lost to progress. While the physical structure of Old Main no longer exists, one hopes its memory will be preserved as a colorful part of our local history.

In March, 1899, a group of Baptists met in Palestine, Texas, to consider establishing a facility for the education of people in East Texas. Jacksonville was chosen for a location and the East Texas Educational Society was granted a charter by the Secretary of State. Eighteen acres were purchased for $1,864.00 and Jacksonville College has been in the same location for one hundred twenty three years. The contract for a building was awarded to local contractors, Edgar Aber and Fredrick Haberle, in May 1899 and Old Main was completed in six months. The structure was three stories and remained on "College Hill" for sixty-eight years.

Old Main was an architectural masterpiece. The structure was 60 feet by 80 feet and was about 45 feet tall not including the bell tower. The bricks used were made by Aber Box and Basket Factory in 1898. A newspaper article at that time stated "these bricks were as fine a brick that ever went into a building." There were 225,000 bricks used in the construction of Old Main. The building did not have foundation or piers but the bricks were laid directly onto the sandy ground. The cornerstone was laid by the Masonic Lodge on November 30, 1899 and Rev. R. C. Burleson, who baptized Sam Houston, gave the dedicatory address. A financial report to the Trustees of Jacksonville College in 1919 indicated the building cost of Old Main was $5,000.00. The building along with the Twin Towers, a similar structure at Lon Morris College, were landmarks for the city. Old Main was the tallest building and could be seen from Seven Mile Hill south of Jacksonville. Jacksonville College began classes in September, 1899, in the Templeton Building on Bolton Street and J. V. Vermillion served as the first President.

Classes were moved into Old Main when it was completed at the end of December. The double stairways on each side of the vestibule of Old Main were separately used by the girls on one side and boys on the other. Mrs. C. R. Jenkins, a former public school teacher in Jacksonville, in 1997 recalled she was reprimanded by President B. J. Albritton for using the boys' stairs. Pranks by students were climbing the fire escape on the outside of Old Main and ringing the bell in the bell tower.

In 1953 Dr. Curtis Carroll, President of Jacksonville College, studied plans for the restoration of Old Main but a restoration was deemed too expensive. In 1968 Gary Arnett, a local contractor who built most of the buildings for Jacksonville College, dismantled Old Main.

Old Main has many personal family ties for me. My father, Rev. Claude E. Banks was Dean of Students and my mother, Laverne L. Banks taught biology for over twenty-five years. I was raised in the neighborhood around Old Main and I proudly graduated from Jacksonville College. My house is built with the bricks from Old Main.

Today the R.C. and Frances Buckner Chapel occupies the location on College Hill but many citizens and former students fondly remember Old Main.

JACKSONVILLE'S 150th CELEBRATION 1872 · 2022

Recollections of Jacksonville

A Memoir by Michael Banks

We Are More Alike Than We Are Different

My name is Elizabeth Boyd Battle; I was born in the Spring of 1957. I am a 65-year-old African American woman, residing in the Mt. Haven community that is approximately 2.5 miles west of Jacksonville. My parents were Ed and Laura Boyd. I was raised in a household with eleven siblings. I have two grown children and four amazing grandchildren named Jeremy Jr, Zackary, Anthony and Riley.

I grew up in a small community called the Sand Pitt. We were poor but when your neighbors' living conditions looked the same, it was normal. I attended Mrs. Clemmons Kindergarten, Elberta Elementary, and Fred Douglass: all black schools during the segregation era. By 1970, all schools had integrated; I remember it being a hard transition for all.

Our childhood was hard, but fun which required chores before and after school. Neighborhood fishing trips were the most exciting days. Summers were filled with responsibilities; we went to the tomato and pea fields. We worked for money, but sometimes for halves. Earning halves ensured us that we would have fresh vegetables for winter.

During my teen years, I vividly remember not being allowed in café dining areas; instead, we went to the back-alley door where the cooks entered and sat in a small dim corner area to be served. We attended the Palace Theatre which was segregated also. The black people were upstairs, and the white people were downstairs. Sometimes milk cartons were accepted for admission. I remember stories of Dr. Martin Luther King Jr, a social rights activist that rallied for African Americans: civil rights, voting rights, fair wages, fair treatment, and other economic injustices.

In 1976, I entered the vocational nursing school, I was the only person of color accepted and I was addressed as a Negress. That was a stressful year for me, but I found a true friend who did not see my color by the name of Sue Price. In 1986, Mt. Haven was almost destroyed by a tornado. Many families lost everything they possessed. Years later the community rebuilt, what was once a predominately black community had transformed into a more diverse community. In 1990, I enrolled in a higher education institution, and I received an Associate Degree in Nursing.

In 2020, the Covid-19 Pandemic spread across the globe. The pandemics rapid surge caused hospital capacities to hit the maximum, and patients were sent either back home, or hundreds of miles away where bed availability could be found, and there were thousands of recorded daily deaths. Due to the consequences of the virulent out of control pandemic, face coverings/mask mandates were implemented; store shelves were stripped of essentials: cleaning supplies, meat, toilet paper, etc.

No matter what the future holds, I pray that our future generations are living in a healthy environment, without racism, injustices, and inequalities. Everyone is not a fan of change or uncertainty, but when we as an individual and as a collective group of people embrace change, it enables all to thrive. Remember that there have been many men and women from every background that have sacrificed everything so you can live with the freedom and the privileges that you have today. We are more alike than we are different.

JACKSONVILLE'S 150th CELEBRATION 1872 · 2022

Recollections of Jacksonville

A Memoir by Elizabeth Battle, RN

Visiting Downtown

Like lots of kids, I grew up in the rural area surrounding Jacksonville, but we "country kids" felt as much attachment to the city proper as the "townies." Jacksonville was not only our education destination, but it was the hub of our shopping and a considerable part of our social interactions and job opportunities.

One of my favorite memories of growing up here was the weekly trip to downtown. Back in the late 60's and early 70's, a good portion of the retail shops were still located downtown on the few blocks along Commerce, Main, Bolton, and Ragsdale Streets. On a Saturday, the atmosphere was downright festive with shoppers crowding the sidewalks, going in and out of stores or clustered underneath the awnings catching up on the latest news. To find a "park" (our term for parking space) was a challenge, and then you had to feed the parking meters. Usually a nickel would buy you enough time to do your business, but sometimes Mama would send me out to put in an extra penny. Few locked their cars back then...you didn't need to. If it was hot and you were fortunate to have air-conditioning in your car (it was optional, not standard like it is now.), you could leave your car running while you dashed into a store to run an errand.

People dressed up to go to town. Ladies wore dresses or nice pantsuits, kids wore their good clothes (rips and tears were not fashionable then), and it was not uncommon to see men in suits and dress hats or pressed slacks and a tie. You went to shop and be seen – it was a social event as well as a practical one. The sights, sounds, and smells I remember as vividly today as a half century ago: the sparkling display of silver and china at Lang's Jewelry, the tantalizing smell of freshly popped popcorn wafting across downtown from Duke & Ayers, the sharply dressed mannequins adorning the windows of Beall's, J.C. Penney's, and J. B. White's department stores, the musty oily smell of Cherokee Hardware where there was a plethora of tools and odds and ends of all sorts, and over all of these floated the echo of the First Methodist Church bells that tolled the hour. At Christmas, piped carols rang out over downtown and brightly decorated windows added to the holiday shopping experience.

Sometimes, after spending several hours browsing and visiting, we would walk to Abell's Pharmacy for lunch or a mid-afternoon treat. On the way, I loved passing the Barber Shop and seeing the twirling red, white, and blue barber pole. It reminded me of a living candy cane. Abell's had a real old-fashioned soda fountain and lunch counter – complete with red vinyl topped metal stools and some booths off to the side. We would order a hamburger or grilled cheese or sometimes just a shake or scoops of ice cream. They made the sandwiches and burgers right behind the counter on an open grill. The shakes were made with a big metal machine with a large stainless steel tumbler that would hold the extra bit of shake after they filled a tall clear glass. Sometimes I shared the extra in the tumbler with Mama or my brother, Josh. It was served with a paper straw and a long-handled spoon. They were so thick and delicious…I'd give a C-note to taste an Abell's vanilla shake again!

Before leaving town, we would usually stop by and see my sisters, Sherry and Melanie, who worked the candy counter at Duke & Ayers. Mama would give us a dime or a quarter to spend, and my brother and I would fill a small paper bag with bubblegum and anything else that struck our fancy. What we got for our dime or quarter would take several dollars to purchase now. When I think back and realize that world we enjoyed is long gone, it makes me a little sad that my children and grandchildren won't experience the joys I remember, but I also know those memories can be an important part of the legacy I share with them…and hopefully, in the sharing, those wonderful places, sights, and sounds will live on to delight new generations.

Recollections of Jacksonville

A Memoir by Tamra McAnally Bolton

Transplanted and Rooted in Jacksonville

My history with Jacksonville began in August, 1963, when our family was transferred by United Gas Corporation from New Braunfels to Jacksonville. Quite a surprise to me being uprooted from the town I was born and lived 14 great years to a town 250 miles away. I had no idea why this was happening and as how could there be a better place than New Braunfels. To say the least I was extremely entrenched where I lived and it was a hard place to leave for so many reasons. The transition had its ups and down for a short time, but there is something about Jacksonville that captured the essence of life with its natural hospitality and easy living in a beautiful area. I have always believed that the town is very much an open community that welcomes those that want to participate. To me, you will not be shut out based on one's pedigree or whether you were born here. Some towns are. There are so many good organizations that welcome the participation from well meaning newcomers without a second thought just glad you are here. The town has a great spirit and always has.

Speaking of spirit, the four years I was at JHS were some of the greatest times of my life. We were blessed with great teachers and leaders in our schools that were particularly interested in the well being of their students in my times there from 1963 to 1967. Four years now goes very fast, but back then it seemed longer, and I enjoyed all the experiences gained in the social, educational, spiritual, recreational, working, athletic, opportunities in our town and the big city of Tyler was there to fill in the gaps. It was a great place at a great time in America.

I really didn't know what my future looked like, and likely because I was enjoying high school now and not looking ahead. One thing that did catch my eye and made a great impression on me was the Jacksonville Chamber of Commerce. What I noticed through the newspaper (daily) was a lot of articles about what was going on in town and for a smaller town that was pretty impressive to me. Economic Development was a main focus of the C of C, and I am sure they had other parts, but this was an impressive group that worked together to make Jacksonville known, and that we would like for your business to relocate here and we could make that happen. I have reason to believe that these men spent a lot of their own money to see about prospects and their interest in our offers.

The paid person was Bob Eitelman, and he was obviously a leader and did wonderful work while here leading the community and setting the pace on trips to Dallas, Houston, and anywhere they were summoned to tell our story. The original Business Park was land North of between Highway 69 and Bolton Street. The land was given and, along with other negotiated terms, there was an explosion of new businesses, mainly manufacturing, that relocated here for reasons presented by this welcoming group led by Bob Eitelman. Each year the Jacksonville Daily Progress would have a section regarding the number of new businesses relocated here. This was impressive to me as there would be 15-25 each year in a variety of businesses, but primarily plastics as that was a growing need and we were helping it grow. One year Paul Harvey (good day!) was the speaker at the annual banquet in the 70's. He was so impressed with our growth for a small town and announced on his extremely popular daily national radio broadcast about Jacksonville. Not a small deal at the time and very true.

Back to me again, as I noticed this progress it made an impression on me. It took leadership to bring in the "economic engine" that was good for the company; but also so good for the town and the people to be employed with steady good paying jobs that brought good things such as jobs, schools, streets and highways, shops, sales of boats, cars, homes, churches, banks, restaurants, etc. and a lot of security for families. I even noticed new classmates were moving here, just like I did, mostly due to this activity that likely brought them here.

JACKSONVILLE'S 150th CELEBRATION 1872 · 2022

Recollections of Jacksonville

A Memoir by Gene Brumbelow

Once an agricultural area, the 60's and 70's were sort of an industrial revolution taking place right here and not many towns can say the same. There was a leader and a good one at that time and no doubt Jacksonville benefitted. The legacy has continued through the years to today with the leadership that emerges every year to volunteer the place that we love and want to make even better for the next Centennial.

The Fabric of Jacksonville History

In the mid-1800s, pioneers were establishing themselves in Cherokee County. In preparation for their trip west they followed printed guidebooks that told them to leave home with plenty of provisions. As a result, a great deal of sewing and quilting was done prior to leaving. Along the way they endured many hardships, spent months in wagons with little time to rest before they reached their destination. Quilts were often used on the trail.

Since the wagons had no suspension and the roads were rough, many people would soften the ride with quilts; wrap family heirlooms such as clocks, and when necessary provide comfort as a woman gave birth during the trip. Once settled in their new homes, women began to gather for quilting bees and sat around a wooden quilting frame hung from the ceiling. Friendship quilts were a favorite, often called autograph quilts because names of the quilters' family and friends were embroidered on the quilt along with meaningful dates. These quilts became keepsakes which functioned as a record of family and community life, to be passed down from generation to generation. In addition, woven coverlets were produced on looms and became indispensable items. Coverlets often incorporated imported indigo and madder dyes, although natural home dyes were used as well. Weavers concocted colors from organic materials like bark, plants, moss, clay, even dried insects.

In 2010, while finalizing my book, Quilts and Their Stories Binding Generations Together, I learned there were still "discoveries" to be made in the Jacksonville area; topics worthy of study, some forgotten for a time, but all inspirational. First is a quilt from the Earle's Chapel community located five miles west of Jacksonville on Hwy 79, and established in 1859. During an interview, Neil Earle shared the following story with me. A 1939 Earle's Chapel Friendship Quilt mysteriously became packing material for furniture and found its way overseas. After 33 years this
'lost' quilt was returned to its rightful place in the community.

Just as pioneers had used quilts as packing material for precious items, movers in Bridge City, Texas, arrived at the home of career Air Force officer Lt. Col. Joe Howard with a quilt to protect goods to be moved. His wife

Jean asked if the movers knew where the quilt was from and they replied, 'no'. Jean Howard asked if she could keep it, and thus began the saga of the quilt that accompanied the Howards on their 12 moves around the globe. The quilt made two trips to Iran, once by ship and once by air. In 1979, it survived the Iranian Revolution in a warehouse that was surrounded by buildings in flames! At an Earle's Chapel reunion June 22, 2003, the 'lost' quilt was finally home and on display; everyone present marveled as Lt. Col Howard told the story.

A second quilt is the 1935 Corine School Quilt made by mothers of students at the time as a going away gift for Mrs. G.H. Thomas, a teacher who taught there from 1927-1935. Unusual in that each block of the quilt contains a student's name, the only adult name present on the quilt is the teacher's. Corine, a farming community eight miles west of Jacksonville, was settled after the Civil War, a post office opened in 1888, and a school was established in 1892. Eventually the school closed and consolidated with Jacksonville. It is not known how this quilt came to be in a Tyler antique store; when in 1980 Mary Taylor, an employee of Jacksonville ISD and member of the Cherokee County Historical Commission, spied it. She explained, "It's a joy to find a piece of history and be part of its return…The friendship quilt caught my eye as I immediately recognized names like Lloyd Bearden and Harold Simpson. I called Virginia, Harold's wife, and she purchased it. Virginia, at the time resided in the Corine Community, smiled as she told me, "I didn't hesitate, didn't ask the price, a first for me! I just bought it…" Other family names on the quilt are Martin, Acker, Bledsoe, Oden, Cooper, and Lockhart, just to name a few.

Quilt number three owned by Shelley Cleaver was made by his mother, Sissie, and her Sunday school class at the First Baptist Church, Jacksonville. All of the class members' names are on the quilt, along with several pastors. Of interest is a block with the embroidered name of Mrs. Eunice Sanborn, a member of the class who was born July 20, 1895. For a time, Eunice would reign as the oldest living person in the US.

Finally, I was told some very old quilts were housed in the Vanishing Texana Museum which was located inside the Jacksonville Public Library where Chick-fil-A is now. I asked, Library Board member, Randy Gorham, if I might see the quilts and include them in my book. I wasn't prepared for what I would find and neither was then Library Director, Mrs. Barbara Crossman. As we carefully examined the four quilts in the collection, we found a note written by Carl Smith which reads, "Dear Elizabeth, These old quilts were brought to Chicago in 1912 from a truck in my step-grandmother's barn, Mrs. Mollie Mitchell, 2nd wife of my maternal grandfather... These are for your museum." (The Elizabeth was Elizabeth (Betty) Brown who married Frank Ebaugh and became curator of the museum section of the library.)

Then as I was about to leave, I noticed something rolled up on a shelf in the back, and asked Mrs. Crossman what that might be. She responded it looked like a hooked rug. As we examined it, a note fluttered out. It read, "Hand-woven coverlet made before 1836 owned by Mrs. Hall, great grandmother of Mrs. E.P. Dolan, Jr. used by Sam Houston while guest in the Hall home." Mrs. Crossman was shocked, had no idea this small collection had such relevance to Texas history.

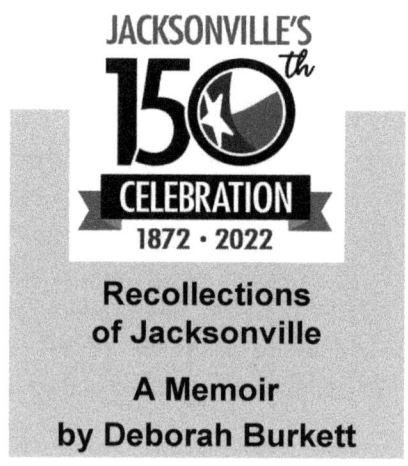

One Hispanic Person's Journey

I came to Jacksonville from Houston, Texas, around 1964-65 with my parents and my four siblings. I was about five or six years old at the time. My step-father was employed by Wing Archery and the company relocated so we followed the company here.

Our first house that we lived in was on Canada Street. At the time there were about only 12 Hispanic families in town. The families were the Trevino's, the Hernandez's, the Meza's, the Verga's, the Mendoza's, the Fuentis', the Lova's, the Prito's, the Maldonado's, and the Varrias'. Some of these families relocated here to work in the fields, being as Jacksonville was the Tomato Capitol of the World. Most of these families decided to stay to continue to work in the fields and raise their families here.

After being here a year or two, our family had moved across town to Alabama Street. I recall a time when we were going to town and we came upon a road block. The city police and immigration officers were doing checks for illegals on Patton Street (Tomato Road) next to the city jail (currently Sadler's Restaurant). They checked my step-father's driver's license, but didn't believe that he was a citizen. They arrested him and took him to jail. There were three kids in the car at the time, and we were scared that we were all going to jail. My mother didn't have a driver's license, so we had to walk home to his my step-father's birth certificate to get him out of jail. A few years later, I asked my older brothers if they had ever worked on Tomato Road packing tomatoes. They stated that they had, and they got paid $0.40 an hour, and worked 10 to 12 hour days. Back then I recall that gasoline prices were $0.43 a gallon in comparison to $3.15 a gallon in 2021.

Our family fished and hunted anything that we could eat to survive almost daily. We fished and hunted at Carey Lake. I recall an Indian cave at Carey Lake that went under the road and came out on the other side. Past that point, there was a wooden bridge that you would have to cross to go further into the woods. The other place we enjoyed to visit was Love's Lookout. We enjoyed going out there and having picnics under the pavilions. There were a lot of things to do out there. They had a swimming pool and an amphitheater. I recall walking up to the swimming pool area and watching certain people swimming, as we weren't allowed to enjoy it ourselves. Not too long after that, the pool was closed because of segregation.

Recollections of Jacksoville

I attended elementary school at East Side, Joe Wright, and West Side Elementary (first and sixth grades). I attended Junior High (7th and 8th grades) at the current location of the Texas National Bank. I attended Jacksonville High School from the 9th to the 12th grade. There were 19 Hispanics attending the high school at that time. When I was a freshman in high school, a friend and I were talking in Spanish to one another. The teacher overheard us and told us that we weren't allowed to talk in Spanish. When I asked why, she simply told me that I just wasn't allowed to do it. There were times that we were disrespected and treated unfairly. There were some good programs in high school. I was a member of the ICT program which allowed you to attend classes for half a day and work the other half of the school day. At that time, I began working for Bernard Mayfield as a painter's helper for 19 years Upon his retirement I began my own business as a paint contractor. I graduated from JHS in 1978. There were five Hispanics in my class, but only two of us graduated; a guy named Ralph Montemayor and me.

In 2000, the Hispanic population was between 34 to 36 percent. In 2011, it was 50.3 percent, and in 2021, it is at 55 percent. IN 2000, I was asked to run for the school board of the Jacksonville ISD and won in which I served nine years. I was the first Hispanic ever to be on the board. I was also appointed by Governor Rick Perry to serve on the Angelina Neches River Authority (ANRA) board, which is Lake Columbia, for 12 years.

We have a lot of small Hispanic businesses that have started up in our community. Some of them are Taqueria Torres, La Juanita, Paco's Tires, La Fond Del sol, Bella Furniture, Gonzales Insurance, Toledo Finance, Jorge Aragon Farmers Insurance, and Supper Gallo Food Store. This is only a few of the businesses. I have been blessed and happy to serve my community. My three children grew up and graduated from here. My son, Cordero, went to Stephen F. Austin University; my daughter, Alayna, went to Texas A & M, and my other soon, Emilio, went to Texas State University in San Marcos.

Recollections of Jacksonville

A Memoir by Al Chavira

Humble Beginning - Paved Road to Gratefulness

Years ago, there was a little Negro girl born as the first of eight children in what she thought was an average family. She did not know her family was considered poor. She was never hungry and always had the best time playing with creative toys and games she and other children in the neighborhood made. Playing games outside and pushing tire casings on the hot sandy lane then resting under tall pine trees and Chinaberry trees made for some of the best days of her life.

The family resided in a community called Mt. Haven, known now as 747 N. An outside restroom, use of lamp lights, and no phone or television was a way of life. The young girl started to school at the age of five. The school, Mt. Haven Elementary, was a three-room house with a kitchen and outside restroom. The school housed first through eighth grades. School staff included three teachers and a cook. Daily lunch consisted of a hot meal at the cost of eleven cents. The youngster wore overalls and cotton stockings to keep warm. She, along with her siblings and other children in the community, walked to school which was about four or five miles away. Mt. Haven Elementary School provided a solid educational foundation for the children in the community and held its first graduation in 1955.

As the young girl grew, it became apparent that she was a good basketball player, even while playing on a dirt court. She entered high school in 1955 at Fred Douglass High School, an all-Black school. Students in Jacksonville ISD were separated by the color of their skin. She also experienced segregation on the streets of downtown Jacksonville. On Commerce Street, water fountains were labeled "White" and "Colored." At the café, coloreds had to use the back door if they wanted to be served.

Following graduation from Fred Douglass High School, she attended Prairie View A&M, a historically black university (HBCU), for two years. She did not know about grants and scholarships. She used book previously used by someone else. She married and had four beautiful daughters and went back to school later to further her education.

I am that young girl, Charlie Mae (Scott) Esco. I am a lifelong resident of Jacksonville, Texas. I grew up thinking there were two worlds, white and black. As I grew older, I realized that all people are just that…people, with different skin color.

It became my goal to support community service in all facets of the community alongside people of all ethnicity and race. I have served as a volunteer fire fighter, worked as a referee for basketball and volleyball in public ISDs, worked as a teacher's assistant and bus driver in JISD, worked for Head Start, completed Citizen Police Academy (twice, the second time at the age of 80), member of Fred Douglass Alumni Association, member of National Council of Negro Women, United Women of Strength, Career Women, served on the Cherokee County Appraisal Review Board, County Historical Commission, and MHMR Board. In some of these organizations, I was the first minority woman. My humble beginning paved the way for a grateful heart. I am truly grateful for my story and give the glory to my Heavenly Father!

Recollections of Jacksonville

A Memoir by Charlie Mae Scott Esco

This is Home

My mom and dad, Wilson and Joyce Folden moved to Jacksonville in 1956 from Nacogdoches. Dad came to work for Nichols-Kusan. They had one daughter, Cindy, already and in the next four years, along came Larry, then me. Once I was school age, mom started her 30+ year career as a teacher at Joe Wright Elementary School. I was lucky enough to have the opportunity to grow up on Deaton Street with great neighbors, which included the Adams, Bolton, Berry, and Gray families. Each of these families had a part in making me who I am today. I'm immensely grateful for the guidance each of them provided. And we cannot forget the Friday night "kick the can" gatherings.

And then there are my Central Baptist Church mom's – Wanda Cummins, Mary Taylor, Tommie Dotson, Jeanette Creed, and Claxene Jay, to name a few. I don't think I realized how pivotal their godly ways would get me through the various "life hurdles" along the way. We walked to East Side Elementary School each day, and even to the junior high when it was "all the way over" on Neches St. That was back in the day when mom's sent kids off telling us "just don't walk home alone," like that was possible with 12 – 15 kids at any given time.

After graduation from Jacksonville High School, I couldn't wait to make my way through Stephen F. Austin State University, and then off to the big city of Dallas. I worked my way into the laboratory diagnostics industry, which is where I met my "Yankee" husband Ed Gellock. He swept me off my feet all the way to life in New Jersey and Pennsylvania. Another you don't realize it at the time moment was when I found a job at a pharmaceutical company. Twenty-nine years later, I'm still finding how important the work we do every day is to people of all walks and ages.

Our ultimate goal was to be back home and live on Lake Jacksonville. In 2014 we made the dream happen and I wouldn't change a thing. I LOVE this town. And now I get to serve my town having been elected to serve as the District 2 City Councilwoman. Sam Hopkins tells me I'm only the third female to be on the City Council, and I think that is pretty cool. For my best friends who make coming home even more special, and the traditions we hold dear to our hearts, it is one of the best decisions I've ever made. Coming home is and was priceless. Happy 150th birthday Jacksonville!

Back in 1972

Looking back to the year 1972, I was 14 years old and present at the Hazel Tilton Park when the time capsule was buried. Also, during 1972, I had just purchased a 1932 Chevrolet 4-door sedan from a gentleman in Troup TX for $ 150.00. Dad and I brought it home on a flatbed trailer, as did not have an engine, or a floorboard! Setting in my garage, I would tinker on it and eventually, Dad and I had it completely restored. It took us 2 years to restore it, which was based on how much money I could earn and have available to spend on my car. I accomplished this by mowing yards all over the east side and having a daily paper route selling the Jacksonville Daily Progress to the patients in Nan Travis Hospital.

Completing the car was a great goal, and as a freshman in high school, this was "my ride". It was complete with white lettered Micky Thompson wide tires, glass packs in the exhaust for that deep, loud roar, and an 8-track player in the dashboard. My after-school plans included a dove hunt with my 20-gauge shotgun in the back seat. Many trucks in the parking lot at the high school had a "gun rack" in the back window, and most had either a shotgun or a rifle in the rack. There was no gun violence or threat of such. We just wanted to go hunting after school!

If shopping was on the agenda, one might go to The Sports Shop to purchase a new baseball. Duke & Ayers was a popular five and dime store across from Austin Bank. If you needed a watch repaired, or some jewelry, The Diamond Shop or Lang's Jewelry were the places to visit. But, after Cheryl and I married after high school, and began our family, we had to sell the old 32 Chevy to help pay the bills. We raised our family here in Jacksonville, and have never lived in any other city. We are both proud of our lifelong heritage here in Jacksonville. Never in my wildest imagination would I have ever guessed that I would have the privilege of serving our citizens as Mayor of our dear City, especially during this exciting time. There are lots of festivities planned for that Sesquicentennial Celebration day on October 22, 2022, and I hope many will "come home" for the celebration.

Recollections of Jacksonville

A Memoir by Randy Gorham

Stripling Farm and the Expansion of the JHS Campus

In 2000 the JISD school board purchased what was known as the Striping Farm which was adjacent to the JHS campus. For some taxpayers, this was seen as a ridiculous amount of money to acquire the acreage. For me, I saw it as a wonderful opportunity to allow for expansion of our "land locked" campus. The following chronicles the events that followed that controversial purchase and reflects the campus in the year 2021.

Each day as I arrive at Jacksonville High School, I have the pleasure of driving down a scenic and aesthetic pathway. The addition of this beautiful drive is an integral part of the recent additions and construction efforts of the JISD school board. A visitor is greeted at the "guard shack" by a gentleman who also monitors unwanted guests. As you look to the left, one will see the new tennis courts, softball diamond, soccer practice field and the cross-country track. Trees were left on the right to buffer adjoining property.

The tennis courts were the first expansion to the land that JISD purchased in 2000 known as the Stripling Farm. As a young girl, I lived on Palestine Street and remember attending day camp at this farm. We thought we were "going to the country" for our camp. This property was the "smoking section" for the students of the 1980's and 1990's. I often saw students running into the woods to be closely followed by a principal. Upon seeing two young boys walking down the street carrying gas cans, I alerted our principal, Roy Darby. Further investigation revealed that they had stolen a four wheeler from Sadler's marine and stashed it in the wooded area. There needed to be a better use for this property.

In 2005, a state of the art field house was added to our campus. Replacing the outdated facility, this gave our athletes access to a weight lifting area as well as modern training facilities. It was built where the old tennis courts were located. The baseball diamond and joining facilities are behind the fieldhouse. Our beloved "happy valley" remained in its location for the arduous journey back to the field house.

Also added to this property was a softball facility, a soccer field and a cross-country track. The land was just the expansion area needed to keep our campus from being land-locked. An attractive fence was added with lights, trees, etc. and is now a showplace for visitors to see when coming onto our campus. The two ponds are another focal point of this area. In addition, the buses now enter and leave by this route, diverting the traffic from Palestine and Henderson streets, a much needed safely feature.

As JHS continued to grow, a new classroom wing was added in 1999 along with a renovation of the main hallway. The new paneling added to the tile that replaced the gravel floors in 1993, complete with Indian heads reflecting our mascot. A much needed gift of a new track and athletic area was added to our campus in 2016. The new multipurpose building was added that same year which is used by the female athletes, cheerleaders and drill team.

Another major project in 2012 completed changed our campus. The new cafeteria, a science wing, and the office area became connected. Gone was the notorius "breezeway". No longer could students put someone's car onto the breezeway as a graduation prank. Students can now cross campus without being affected by the weather. It is a beautiful glass -enclosed facility that seats 750 students. The "dungeon" is now newly remodeled English classes, and our band revived the old cafeteria into three separate band halls (much needed as our band program continues to grow at JHS).

Perhaps the needed CTE addition was one of the most impressive additions to the JHS campus. Many new technologies in welding and a plethora of health, agriculture science and other classes rounded out our last expansion in 2017. We still repair small engines, but are equipped with capabilities of filming the process. Although the location of JHS has not changed, the beauty of our campus has been greatly enhanced by these additions.

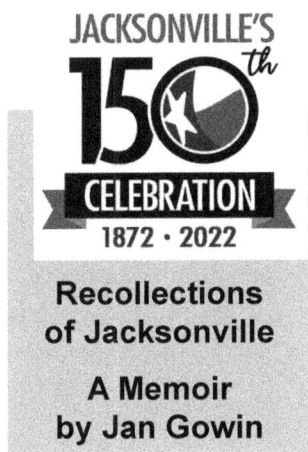

Recollections of Jacksonville

A Memoir by Jan Gowin

Recollections of Jacksoville

A Fond Farewell

I said farewell to another old friend today…

The service was at 10:30 this morning. I had debated even going…. back and forth, back and forth for several days…tormented by the indecision.
In the end, the impulse to go, was somehow stronger than the one to stay.
As I sat there in the old pew, looking around at this familiar place, once again admiring the workmanship here that has always intrigued me as far back as I can remember… The gentle curve of the plaster, arched across the vaulted ceiling, how it was painstakingly sculpted to meet the majestic columns that brace the massive roof, the wide plank windowsills, that until recently held the fabulous nearly two-storied, stained glass windows, now installed in the "new" building, all the things I know so well, and have studied so intensely on more occasions than I can count….

And even so, again I find myself appreciating what I see before me this morning. The old girl still resonates with a timeless beauty; the only visual aberrations are ones that have appeared in the most recent years: strange wires and cords to meet technology needs, neglect from her current occupants, once the decision to leave was finally made. But still she maintains a sort of regal majesty, too well orchestrated a hundred years before to be obscured even now…. the bones are still there, and they are good bones…

The First United Methodist Church began here in Jacksonville in the 1850's, moving to this building in 1908. Today, the Assistant Minister asks for a show of hands, first – for those of a second generation, then a third, a fourth, and last a fifth. I didn't raise my hand… somehow, I just could not….

Some member of my family has attended this church since the mid-1860's, and now with my granddaughter, at least six generations of Trotters and Walkers have sat on these very pews, in this very room. I think of those that were here before me, of their faith, of their vision and determination to erect a building like this back then…. The architect in me knows it would be impossible today…. The craftsmen no longer exist, or the astronomical cost, prohibitive, even if some could be found.

I think of the multitude of occasions when my family has gathered here… I imagine the christenings my great grandparents, and aunts and uncles had… the funerals, the meetings, the weddings, the revivals, the speakers, the communions, the parties, the Easter and Christmas services.... An almost endless series of events, more than my mind can absorb....

I remember those of my own: sitting on a different pew, my legs stretched out across the seat, not quite reaching the edge of it.... The tiny white shoes I wore under some frilly dress they insisted I wear.... transforming me for a few moments, from the wild indian/cowgirl, girl-child I normally was, into some doll-like creature they thought I should be....., my grandmother sticking out her lower teeth in fun, so that only I can see.... making me laugh, keeping me occupied there in that pew, when all I can think about, is the fried chicken, mashed potatoes, the homemade yeast rolls and thick cream gravy, and big glasses of iced tea, waiting at home, and how fast I would get out of these stiff leather shoes!

I look up to the huge balcony, above us, wishing I was big enough to be up there with the older kids, intuitively knowing the fun and mischief going on up there....I think about later, when I moved to Jacksonville as an adult, and stood at this altar rail, holding the tiny hands of my children as they were baptized and we were received into this church.... I remember Raymond Teague, coming up there to stand with us, welcoming us that day...
I remember how I watched these children learn to be Acolytes and how proud I was... I remember the field trips, the parties, Sunday school, the year I taught my youngest' fifth grade class, and how I agonized over the lessons... I think about MYF, sex-education classes, Lakeview Camp, the scavenger hunts, the egg hunts, the canned food hunts, the pot-luck suppers, the Easter and Christmas Communions, and their High School graduation services...

I think of that magical evening, just three years ago, when I walked with my oldest child, arm and arm, down this center aisle, at her wedding, to a waiting young man, she'd known through this church since fourth grade.... So many memories, here in this fine, grand, old room.... And I reflected on these things, here, this morning, counting in my mind's eye, all the moments collectively shared here, and the people I have known in these hallowed halls...

People who mentored me, a young, single mother, in this sometimes, backward country town.... Realizing that most of them are gone now, too: Hazel Decker, Mary Elba Brown, Barbara Green, Charles Ross, Ruth Alexander, Mary Arnett, Raymond Teague, and Darrell Porter to name just a few...people who were larger than life, each unique, committed by faith.... I'm grateful for their patience with me and more than that, I appreciate the opportunity I had to spend time with this treasured group. I feel strongly their presence here today, giving me the strength I'll need to complete this mission.

I think for a moment about the music I've enjoyed here.... How I learned to play "Amazing Grace" on the piano there in the old Alpha-Omega Sunday school room, long before my feet could touch the pedals....
I think of the words heard spoken here: the announcements, the speeches, the prayers and requests...

I grew up hearing the names of Methodist preachers mentioned on a daily basis, starting with stories about my own great grandfather, George Washington Trotter, a lay Methodist preacher on the East Texas Circuit. Over the years I met or heard speak most of the living ones all over the South, and many of them at this very pulpit. Some of the John Towers even roomed for a while in my grandmother's home. She used to tell us stories about the games she played as a child, coming to Texas in a covered wagon, the tenth of nineteen children. One of her favorite games, she told us, was "playing preacher". When asked how this was done, she would reply that "she would climb up on some old nearby stump and go to preachin'", expecting us to know just what the heck she was talking about! This thought reminds me now of the sermons I have heard here..., some more effective than others....
I think of Matt Idom and one of his best.... The one with the rooster crowing, in the distance at the very end... a powerful moment for those of us here that morning, and for me especially, as one artist immediately recognizing another...one with an incredible gift, right up there before me....

I listen now, this morning to Faulk Landrum, find just the perfect words to transition this group to a major new beginning, in another place, far removed from here, knowing this mission can't be easy for him either....

I slowly look around this old room, taking it all in at once, knowing it's for the last time in its current context, and hear these final words spoken, something called "The Declaration of Departure": "This building, having been consecrated and named the First United Methodist Church of Jacksonville, together with the land on which it stands and all objects remaining in it, we now depart and release it for any honorable use. We declare that it is no longer the place of meeting of a United Methodist Congregation"....... Powerful and poignant words... I feel an enormous catch, down deep in my soul, feel the sharp sting, behind eyes starting to fill, mentally resisting, kicking and screaming NO!!.... and then it is over.... as if the plug has been pulled on a dying loved one, the last gasping breath expelled....the one that was... is no more....

We all rise and walk away....through doors we've all entered a thousand times, not looking back.... And not unlike some hospital corridor, each with his own thoughts, and me, with mine...As I write these meager words, feeling a lot like I did on the day of my father's passing, so grateful.....I had this time in this special place.... realizing how rare the total experience has been.... that I was so fortunate to have this history... this connection.... within these ancient walls. Knowing also that had I not been so distracted, admiring this building and her mighty timbers, that perhaps, I'd have been a better shepherd, and the thought humbles me.

But today I know I made the right decision....that my obligation runs too deep to have missed it....my mission has been accomplished, and for all those who came before me, I say with a full heart..... Fare the well, old friend....God's speed....

You were one hell of a church! AMEN!!!

Recollections of Jacksonville

A Memoir by Pat Walker Graham

The Livestock Market

Much has been written about the tomato era in Jacksonville and it was quite enjoyable to read. However, another enterprise was also important near the town. It was located first on Highway 79 West of town, then later, on Highway 79 East of town – that being the Jacksonville Livestock Market. According to the late Audry Owens, manager in the 1970's, 15 million dollars' worth of cattle were sold there in 1973 – one of the best years ever in the cattle business. He also stated that 60,000 head of cattle were run through there each year. (According to a Daily Progress article and a photo from about 1975)

My father and family bought and sold cattle there after the Fort Worth Stockyards era declined. Gooseneck trailers with cattle were lined up out to the road before they were tagged and unloaded. In the café they had hamburgers, chicken fried steaks, fresh vegetables, homemade pies and hot coffee. As a young boy, I got paid a nickel to bring a hot cup of coffee to buyer, Adolf Dotson, who always sat in a comfortable buyer's seat around the front row where the "Holman Boys" would let you know they were at the Jacksonville Livestock Auction.

About fifty years ago, I wrote a song about the business because I was always amazed at other things that went on Saturday's there. Craftsmen were selling their wares and local felt hat maker, Grady Nutt sold his hats there off the tailgate of his pickup truck. My father bought hats there during those years. Old men sold whittled walking sticks and braided whips. They chewed tobacco where they sat outside on long benches in the front of the sale barn, where they talked politics. The "Watkins Man" a tall guy with a small brim hat sold mentholated salve anywhere he could find a buyer inside the auction.

 I hope you enjoy the lyrics of my song and I wish you could hear the melody which is set to kind of the roll of the auctioneer. The song is dedicated to my father the late Clavis Greenwood who was a long time cattleman in this area.

"THE JACKSONVILLE AUCTION"

They make top-notch deals
And cook country meals
At Jacksonville's Livestock Auction

Chew that tobacco and pop that whip
Open that gate and get a good grip
Get you some of that coffee and take you a sip
At the Jacksonville Livestock Auction

They got cedar post and goose neck trailers
They know all the men that's got hay balers
And some of those folks kinda cuss like sailors
At the Jacksonville Livestock Auction

There's some old men there sellin' walkin' sticks
And some sitin' on benches , picken off seed ticks
Some come there just to talk politics
At the Jacksonville Livestock Auction

You might find you a good Bremer bull
A buyer for your cows, if you got enough pull
Or buy 'em some hay to get 'em real full
At the Jacksonville Livestock Auction

They got pickups parked plum out to the road
Straw hats and boots look like a dress code
They yell "tag' em boys and let em unload"
At The Jacksonville Livestock Auction

They run 'em down the alleys 'til they get 'em in a pen
Around twelve o'clock, they start to bring 'em in
So hold onto your hat, if you ain't never been to
The Jacksonville Livestock Auction

There's an old plug horse, a second-hand saddle
Home-made pie, a thousand head of cattle
When the biddin' begins, boy what a battle
At the Jacksonville Livestock Auction

The Auctioneer says all they need's a good home
Just put 'em on some grass and leave 'em alone
And a year from now, they'll be full grown
At the Jacksonville Livestock Auction

There's feeder yards biddin' cross-bred calves
And good ole boys tradin' on the halves
And a remedy man sellin' mentholated salve
At the Jacksonville Livestock Auction

Well forty, now forty, now forty, now half
One, now two, now three, don't laugh
Boys did you ever see such a calf
At the Jacksonville Livestock Auction

Recollections of Jacksonville

A Memoir by James O. Greenwood

A Good Place to Write a Song

I'm not a native of Jacksonville, Texas, but as they say, "I got here as fast as I could." However, I'm a native of Texas, born in Grapeland and raised in Pasadena. During my years in the Houston area, my family spent a lot of time visiting East Texas because my parents were from Grapeland and Elkhart. While growing up in Pasadena, I always dreamed of living in East Texas.

That dream didn't come true until the summer of 1973 when my wife and I moved to Jacksonville. My brother, Tommie, is a minister. He and his wife had moved here in 1969 so he could attend the local Baptist Seminary. Tommie and I had grown-up playing guitars and singing together. We had begun performing Christian music at the youth revivals and camps where he was asked to speak during the period from 1970 – 1973. The schedule increased from a part-time to a full-time one, so my wife and I decided to relocate here.

Before moving here, I had written only one song – that being a lyric rewrite of a then popular song. I hadn't yet tackled the combination of writing original lyrics and music; that's a much more complicated task. From 1973 to 1978, Spirit and Understanding was a full-time ministry. After about a year, the ministry remained S & U, Inc. and the band was named Damascus Road. The band was more of a contemporary Christian rock band. During those years, the five members of the band all began contributing original songs to the band's repertoire.

After the band dissolved, I became more aware of the musical heritage that was a part of the Jacksonville area. I worked in construction and manufacturing positions for the next twenty years and performed as a part-time musician. Not being a prolific writer, I only wrote songs when the inspiration came along. I still prefer quality over quantity; I would rather write a "good" song than just "another" song.

Hopefully I have been successful at that. You be the judge! Visit my website at www.johnniehelm.com. You can listen to the songs from my most recent CD "Foolish Man." The basic tracks were recorded at Duo Studios, a demo recording studio that my brother and I built here in 1983.

You can also find me on www.reverbnation.com/johnniehelm. For me, Jacksonville has been and still is "a good place to write a song!"

It Began With Tennis

When my career brought me to East Texas in 1976, we chose to live in Jacksonville because the high school had a strong tennis program under Coach Tony Harrison. Our older daughter, Jeannie, had lettered twice in tennis at her previous high school and wanted to play on a good team. Sure enough, she and Judy Womack won the district doubles championship for JHS in the spring of 1977. After graduation, because of her record at JHS, Jeannie got to play in the starting lineup of the East Texas State University tennis team. The school has subsequently been renamed Texas A & M at Commerce. My wife and I played tennis too. We were involved in forming the Jacksonville Tennis Association (JTA) in May, 1977.

Back in the early days of the JTA, we got acquainted with many of the business and professional people of town in matches on the four old tennis courts at JHS. At that time, the courts were cracked and the fences were set too close to the courts. High bounding balls could go over the fence sometimes. Nevertheless, there were crowds of people waiting to take turns playing there. Later, in the 1990s six new courts were built at the Middle School, and in 2003 eight championship courts were built at JHS. The four old high schools were replaced by parking lots. The whole time the JTA sponsored many playing events that were eventually recognized in 2004 by the USTA Texas Section as the Best Middle Sized Community Tennis Association in Texas.

Around 2005, my wife Patsy was playing on tennis teams with Fredia Melvin, whose husband was on the city council. Kenneth Melvin would eventually be elected the city mayor. Fredia told Patsy that the City Library Board needed to add a new board member. Fredia asked me if I would accept nomination for appointment to that board. Being a boy who can't say no, I began serving in the city's civic life. While serving on the city library board, I became a life member of the Friends of the Library that was, and still is, ably led by Gordon Bennett. I also helped attorney Joe Angle revive the Jacksonville Library Association, and became an officer on its board of directors. During one of the 2008 city library board meetings, I heard Nancy

Sonntag discuss the program services available through the Jacksonville Literacy Council. The next thing I knew I was the President of the Literacy Council board of directors for eight years from 2009 to 2017.
Meanwhile the City Library Board heard reports from head librarian Barbara Crossman that the library needed more floor space. I suggested that the Vanishing Texanna Museum be moved out of the library and back to the building from whence the library and museum had been located prior to 1983. As often happens to people who suggest projects, I became in charge of relocating the museum to the Senior Building at the corner of Larissa and Bolton streets. In 2011 the city council created the new Vanishing Texanna Museum Board of Directors. Guess who had to head the brand new board? Yep, the boy who just couldn't say no ended up holding the office through 2014. In order to move the museum, the Senior Building had to be internally partitioned into a secure area to protect the valuable museum artifacts. I worked with Greg Lowe in the City Public Works Department, the city manager Mo Raissi, and the Library Association to fund and build the renovation project. The new museum was dedicated in 2014, and I moved on to other things. Have I mentioned that throughout this period of time, my wife and I were still joyously playing on Jacksonville tennis league teams. She was on four teams that won state titles. My fabulous doubles partner, Burt Gabbert, and I were on the famous Tie Dye Guys teams that won eleven state tennis team titles. You just can't let business interfere with your favorite sport now can you.

As a result of having worked closely with the city manager on the museum project, I got nominated for election to the Cherokee County Appraisal District board of directors. I got elected four times and served for eight years on the board, 2014-2021. I learned all about the property valuations that were made for the County Commissioners Court, the city councils, and school districts. I was greatly impressed with how Chief Appraiser Lee Flowers and his staff did their complicated work. After this public service, in 2021 I was appointed by the Jacksonville City Council to chair the City Sesquicentennial Celebration Committee.

The committee members, Deborah Burkett, Charlie Esco, Cassie Devillier, Johnny Helm, Kathleen Stanfill, and Tracy Wallace, with the help of City Communications Director Daniel Seguin and City Manager James Hubbard, have organized a grand city festival for the week of October 16-22, 2022. I am grateful that my tennis interests led to all of these community activities, especially the City Sesquicentennial celebration.

See you there, my fellow citizens of the city I love most.

Fondly Recalling the Past

About Lon Morris College:
I thought Lon Morris College would be forever. My husband Gordon Hugghins and I (Barbara Angelo) met at LMC and married in 1950 after we completed our two years there. All our children and several grandchildren attended LMC. They participated in children's theater, choir, and band. The family all enjoyed theater, choir, and basketball games there. Lon Morris was a powerful influence in our town, in the state and beyond - through the teachers, ministers, business men and women, sports figures and entertainment stars who attended LMC. Lon Morris introduced international students to our area - students from Puerto Rico, Iran, Africa, Asia, and Hispanic countries. There were many close ties to the United Methodist Church. Education at LMC provided personal attention to relationships and encouragement sometimes not found in schools (small campus, but large influence). Through financial difficulties and disaster, many of us remained loyal Bearcats with green and white running through our veins.
Lon Morris closed in 2021 to our great regret.

About the Three Hundred Block of East Commerce Street, Jacksonville:
The 300 block of East Commerce in the 1940's to the 1960's was a part of our family history. Starting on the corner was the Texas State Bank and the Acker Family (Tom and the Colonel.) Going east was the Ross Dorbandt Insurance and Real Estate business. Next down the block came the Nichols Studio with Leonard and Lula Hugghins, Marian Davis, Barbara and Gordon Hugghins, and Myrtle Foreman in the photography business. Then came the Mr. and Mrs. Carl Gray Electric business. Next came Mrs. Jones and Banty at the Cab Stand. Across the street was the McCarroll Chevrolet business (Hugh, Edwin and Jack McCarroll). Next came the Stone Law firm with W. E. Stone, Emerson Stone, Richard Stone, and Sylvia Chitwood. Located next was the Raymond Anderson Furniture store (parents and four sons). On the corner was Charlie Nix and the Western Auto Supply These were mostly all family owned and run businesses. Before air conditioning, attic fans sucked in dust and dirt as the doors were left open. Parking meters required hourly attending. There were no Dairy Queens or McDonalds; so everyone went

home for lunch. There was much going in and out of these businesses by owners and customers. So we waved and chatted and checked on each other daily. The 300 block of East Commerce was family and friendly.

About H.O.P.E (Helping Others Pursue Excellence):
Our community has a caring heart and has helped indigents, the helpless, the homeless, the hungry, and transients for many years. At one time, the churches and individuals donated money and food to these needy ones. The ministers and, perhaps, the United Fund had an account at the First National Bank, which became the Austin National Bank. Frank Waggoner administered these funds as directed by the ministers. At one time, Harold Lansford headed up the Ministerial Alliance. It became obvious that we needed a central agency and HOPE was born from there. My memories of the beginnings of HOPE include hiring Fran Daniel as the first Executive Director. Her office was a desk and telephone in the Radio Station on Nacogdoches Street. Several interested individuals, including Marge Avera and Barbara Hugghins, went with Fran, to visit PATH in Tyler to learn how to begin. We especially wanted help with a food pantry as we combined with the Manna Pantry which was the Ruby Bruno food closet from the First Presbyterian Church. Then we visited soup kitchens in Longview and Palestine for models of feeding people. Our soup kitchen began very modestly at the North Bolton Christian Church by serving Crock Pot soup and often Sandwiches and chips to a small group of ten people. From such humble beginnings, we grew and expanded to many more clients and many more programs. Many organizations, individuals and churches have been very supportive of HOPE and their clients and their needs.

JACKSONVILLE'S 150th CELEBRATION 1872 · 2022

Recollections of Jacksonville

A Memoir by Barbara Angelo Huggins

WHY JACKSONVILLE IS A GREAT PLACE TO CALL HOME!

Jacksonville and East Texas are growing! People are escaping hectic city life from not only Houston and Dallas, but other population dense regions. As people now know they can work from home, so a smaller community is more appealing. They can relocate a business with help from the Jacksonville Economic Development Corporation (JEDCO) and retire to a peaceful lifestyle with scenery truly best described as God's country. Below are some compelling reasons to make Jacksonville your home:

- Friendly and genuine people
- Beautiful rural area with rolling hills, pine trees and plentiful lakes. Loves Lookout has a 35 mile view!
- Low cost of living, relative to the "Big City"
- Great schools with first rate teachers
- Quaint downtown shopping with fantastic local restaurants – Sadler's, Ritual's, The Patio, Commerce Street Drafthouse, Mariscos and Neighbors Coffee
- No city traffic gridlock
- First rate hospitals, UT Health and Christus Trinity Mother Frances
- Strong community of faith with many churches
- Opportunities to volunteer your time where your efforts make a real difference in bettering our community
- Small town life where a diverse population lives and cares for each other
- Jacksonville College, an affordable, convenient and first rate 2 year college, stressing a faith based learning environment
- Great City government that is forward thinking and run by a group of some of our best leaders!
- 70+ industries with a stable manufacturing base that give us a strong economy
- A Chamber of Commerce that is the heart and soul of our community always helping promote our businesses. Equally important is JEDCO and their investment into the community
- Rich traditions – The Tomato Bowl, Tops In Texas Rodeo, Tomato Fest, MLK Parade, Christmas Parade and many others..

- Lake Jacksonville, one of the most beautiful and scenic lakes in the state
- Short drive to Tyler and 2+ hours to Dallas, Houston and Shreveport
- Cherokee County airport with very affordable fuel making easy private access to our area
- River Run Mud Park for 4-wheeling adventure
- Finally, Norman Rockwell's artwork, The Andy Griffith Show, Petticoat Junction and Green Acres all roll up together to me best describing our slice of East Texas. I am sure there are countless other reasons to call Jacksonville/East Texas home. Feel free to add to my list. Come join us, you will be glad you did.

My heartfelt gratitude goes to Jeff Austin, Jr, Sissy Austin, and Jeff Austin 3rd for the work opportunities I have enjoyed here. They each demonstrate a servant's heart in support of Jacksonville and the East Texas community. Their influence has inspired me over the years, to volunteer and make a positive difference.

I am proud to call Jacksonville home for 32+ years.

Recollections of Jacksonville

A Memoir by Nathan Jones

A Career In Education

I was born at the Newborn Hospital in Jacksonville on April 27, 1946. I was the second child of John and Hazel Lester, and had a sister, Sylvia who was ten years older. We lived on a farm south of Rusk, where we raised cows, chickens, and pheasants. Dad was the manager for the Southwestern Electric Service Company. My mother worked for the Texas Education Agency at the Rusk State Hospital.

The Rusk I.S.D. provided me with a very good educational foundation. I graduated in 1964 in a class 64 students. In high school I enjoyed being a member of the band and ran track. As a teen I worked at Brookshire Brothers food store, and at the Rusk State Hospital in the maintenance department. After graduating from Stephen F. Austin University with a degree in secondary education and majoring in social studies, my wife Molly and I lived in Beaumont, where I taught at David Crockett Junior High.

It was only a few months later that I was notified that Uncle Sam wanted me. After considering all of my options, I decided to join the United States Air Force. It was only a few more months later that I was teaching English language to Vietnamese officers in the Republic of Vietnam Language Defense School. After the officers learned enough English, they were sent to bases in the USA to become pilots. While at the Defense School, I also served as an M-60 machine gunner for the Ground Defense Force. After my year long tour of duty was completed, I was
re-assigned to the Brooks Air Force Base in San Antonio to be a sound specialist for the School of Aerospace Medicine Motion Picture Production Unit. It was very interesting to see the advancements that were being made in the field of medicine.

After completing my tour of duty in the Air Force, Molly and I returned to Jacksonville to raise our family. For a short time I worked at the Texas Bank and Trust before becoming a teacher for the Jacksonville Independent School District. I drove a bus, taught government, and economic classes. I continued my education by returning to S.F.A. for a master's degree, and principal's and superintendent's certifications. I held several administrative positions and retired as the Principal of the Compass Center. During part of my education career, I taught economics, government, and history class at Jacksonville College.

Through the years, Molly and I have been active members in the First United Methodist church, serving on many committees, teaching Sunday School classes, and singing in the choir. I've also enjoyed being a Scout Master in the Boy Scouts; secretary and treasurer for 35 years in the Jacksonville Lions Club; member of the Rodeo Association and other community groups.

In conclusion, we have been blessed to raise our children, Matthew, Jeffery, and Stephanie, in the friendly and caring of city of Jacksonville.

Jacksonville, Old to New, 1847-1872

It's late in the year 1847 and we're standing in the middle of a small east Texas town called Gum Creek, taking its name from a nearby stream. Dusk is gathering and a group of the town's founding fathers are huddled by a fire in front of Tom Dean's general store. It's easy to spot some familiar faces; Mr. Ragsdale, Mr. Templeton, and Mr. Earle, along with many others, are talking about the future of their community.

Approaching the group is Mr. Jackson Smith, the future namesake of the town. A former Texas Ranger who guarded Santa Anna until General Houston could take custody of him, Smith had come to this area in search of the Indians who, at the time, were believed responsible for the Killough Massacre in 1838. He loved the area, returns in early 1847, and after opening his blacksmith business, uses his Texas Army land grant to formally layout the new town.

Mr. Smith is also the postmaster of Gum Creek and in his hand is an important document. He hands the document to Mr. E.A. Ragsdale who looks down at the envelope soiled by the blacksmith hands of Mr. Smith. Inside is news that in 1848 Gum Creek will be made a voting precinct with Mr. Ragsdale as the election officer. This letter is confirmation of the town's solid growth and dynamic future.

The town continues to grow and in 1850 changes its name to Jacksonville. Mr. Earle lists 48 business firms in his mercantile record of the new town. The first three on the list were general mercantile businesses located in log buildings around the town square. The same year Joseph Turney opens the town's first hotel. The Methodists and the Baptists have already built their churches and the Presbyterians have plans to break ground on theirs shortly. A new school opened in 1849.

Little did the citizens know that beneath their optimistic outlook resided the economic structure that would end their prosperity. The driver of Jacksonville's economy was cotton and the economic basis of cotton was slavery. In 1850, one-third of the population of Cherokee County was held in slavery. Records show there were only two free Black men.

Abraham Lincoln was elected president in November, 1860 and South Carolina secedes immediately from the Union. Its governor, Francis Pickens, along with his wife Lucy Holcomb Pickens (born in Marshall, Texas) invites other states to join them in a new Confederacy. In January, 1861, Mr. Peter G. Rhome, a respected merchant in Jacksonville, travels to Austin to represent the community at the Citizen's Convention. There, despite the almost super human effort of Governor Sam Houston to turn the tide of public opinion, Mr. Rhome casts his vote, along with others, for succession.

Though it was generally believed that the war would end quickly and that "only a thimble full of blood would be spilled," that was not the case. News soon arrived that the blood of many men of Jacksonville and Cherokee County had been spilled. For all practical purposes, business in Jacksonville came to a standstill. Many businesses closed never to reopen again - their owners never returned. Women and children are left to tend the farms and plantations, a job for which they had no experience. Although the war eventually ends, it is replaced by the horrors of the Reconstruction Era. Attempts to restart businesses are foiled by marauding Confederate soldiers who have no home and no place to find employment.

Slaves, released by the resolution now commonly called "Juneteenth," have few choices. Some set up new towns called Freedom Colonies, towns that still dot the east Texas landscape today. Others sign on as sharecroppers, working the land of those that had enslaved them. Hope is renewed when word finally comes that the International Railroad has signed a contact with Palestine, TX to be the new headquarters of a railroad to be built from Houston to Canada. Ragsdale and Smith try to negotiate locating a station in their town, but the hard scrap of iron ore in the ground makes it too expensive. The railroad surveyors tell the town that the railroad will miss Jacksonville by two miles.

Ragsdale and Smith continue to negotiate with the railroad. Banking on the potential of large agricultural shipments, and with a donation of land by Sarah Fry, the railroad agrees to build a station and plot out a town. On

August 5, 1872, construction crews and the first work engines reach the new community. The rush is on as every business in old Jacksonville loads up its buildings and inventory to move to new Jacksonville. On November 23, 1872, when the first passenger / freight train steams into town, the new community is on hand to greet them. We hope you will visit your Vanishing Texana Museum during this sesquicentennial year to hear more about the dynamic history of Jacksonville. The museum is open every Thursday, Friday, and Saturday from 11 – 4. Free admission at our 302 South Bolton location.

JACKSONVILLE'S 150th CELEBRATION
1872 · 2022

Recollections of Jacksonville

A Memoir by Larry Lydick

Moving Forward, Making Strides

I moved to Jacksonville in 1982 – 40 years ago, and came to work for Beall's department stores. Being a damn Yankee who grew up in Upstate New York, and having always lived in large cities, Jacksonville was quite a change. Small town cultures are quite different from the big city life style that I was used to. In small towns people go out of their way to avoid argumentative conversations because they see each other every day and don't want the friction. In big towns we could argue like cats and dogs during the business day, but after five p.m. we'd all get together for a drink and have great conversation.

Jacksonville has come a long way since 1982. In keeping with Martin Luther King's desire to see us judge each other by the content of our character and not the color of our skin, Jacksonville has made great progress. When I began managing residential properties in the early '90s, I had a client who did not want me to lease to "colored" people. Needless to say I did not take on that person's properties. Just a few years ago, Doctor Michael Banks and I went to have supper at Chili's. It happened to be the night of the Junior Prom or the Senior Ball. There were several bi-racial couples who came to eat, and it just tugged at my heart strings that these kids cared about who each other as a person and not what color each other was. A couple of years ago, when Jacksonville had a memory march in recognition of George Floyd's loss due to a police officer's misconduct, we were a diverse group in that march; we cared about each other.

Ethnically, Jacksonville's largest population is Hispanic, representing 42.9% of us; the white population is 34.5%; the African-American population is 20.3%; and 2.3% represent all other ethnicities. From a manual labor standpoint, the Hispanic population is the backbone of the community. In any regard, the different groups are getting along with each other, and we are no longer seeing neighborhoods that are strictly of one ethnicity. It all gets back to content of character and not skin color.

In May of 2018, Jacksonville made a great stride when Greg Smith was brought on board as city manager. Greg was basically the first city manager to put Jacksonville on the road to progress. Greg was a very forthright man who addressed those issues that Jacksonville needed to work on. During

Recollections of Jacksoville

Greg's tenure Jacksonville budgeted for the new Jacksonville Public Safety facility on South Bolton. It is an awesome facility and demonstrates Jacksonville's progress.

We lost Greg to another city in June of 2021, and were fortunate enough to replace him with James Hubbard, who is continuing in Greg's aggressive and progressive path. James is a heck of a diplomat. James had been president of JEDCO and, when he became the city manager, Shane Pace became the new JEDCO president and continues on James' positive path. Beginning with Greg, continuing with James and including the current city council, with Mayor Randy Gorham, Joe Williams, Police Chief, and Randall Chandler, Director of Public Works, Jacksonville has the best city administration it has ever had. These are the very people who are responsible for the economic growth of Jacksonville.

As a community we all need to come together and stay together to help us stay on the right path...and we are succeeding.

Attractions Lost to Time, Not Memory

When I moved to Jacksonville in the summer of 1968, many things were different and a few have not changed. Some of this change was good but a lot of yesterday was and is missed today.

Railroads were very important and very visible. The Highway 69 overpass had not been built yet, so several times a day, all traffic on U.S. 69 stopped both directions waiting for the train to clear the highway. Also, the Cotton Belt Railroad bisected the City Park block diagonally between the Fire Station and the former Public Library, which now is home to the Vanishing Texana Museum. The effect of that route was to stop all traffic on Larissa, the former U.S. Hwy 79, Bolton and Rusk Street while we waited for the Cotton Belt train to clear that block.

Other things I remember about the railroad tracks in that part of town were the Third Saturday Trade Days which occurred along the tracks before they crossed Bolton Street. You could buy most anything and I definitely found some treasures. Also, there was always a card table with four rickety chairs ready for the daily game of dominoes, 42 most likely.

When Amtrak took over passenger rail service, we lost the passenger train stop made in Jacksonville. Before that, my children and I could board the northbound train, ride all night for a visit with my parents in Michigan. It was a wonderful way to travel with children as they had plenty of room to move around and the clickety-clack of the wheels on the track would lull anyone to sleep. The return trip arrived back in Jacksonville about 7:30 a.m, so breakfast in the dining car was something to look forward to.

Several more things changed or disappeared. The Liberty Hotel was the meeting place for service clubs and Sunday dinner. It was quite elegant but unfortunately burned to the ground shortly after I moved here. Sadler's Restaurant, owned by Monk and Elizabeth Sadler was a fixture for many years and today, their grandson, Rob Gowin, has carried on their great tradition. I remember eating the Blue Plate Special for a dollar back then. Their pies were spectacular then and still are today, thanks to their daughter, Jan Gowin.

Love's Lookout was at its present location, but was the forerunner of our beautiful facility now. The old native rock visitor's center stood where the beautiful new one attracts visitors. The swimming pool was still in use 50 years ago for at least another 10 years but fell into disrepair and the tornado finished it off. A big loss was the beautiful amphitheater which was just south of the visitor center. It had a stage where plays, concerts and Easter Sunrise services were held. I attended a July 3rd Freedomfest Concert in 1974. Sadly, the next year, there was a great disturbance at that site and the beautiful native rock gradually loosened and washed down the hillside. There is now a chain link fence preventing people from experiencing harm by exploring the ruins. You can still see a couple rows of seats just past the standing posts. The view still remains and is enjoyed by locals and travelers alike.

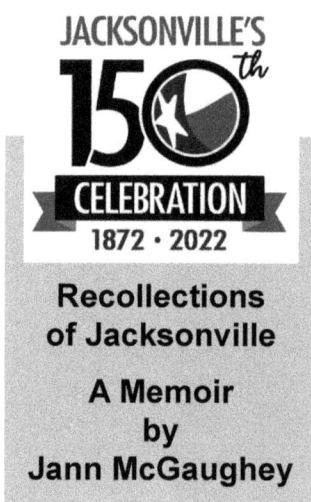

JACKSONVILLE'S 150th CELEBRATION
1872 · 2022

Recollections of Jacksonville

A Memoir by Jann McGaughey

A Comfortable Way of Life

The 1970's was the time I returned to my goals and the business world. Things were still the same with the Vietnam War - messed up in Washington D.C. with more of the same. Five years earlier, we departed for a simpler life fifty miles from Houston to be near a small town and raise our family. The people were friendlier working together on local problems, schools teaching the 3-R's, churches, rodeo, football games Thursday and Friday nights, and hunting and fishing. Taking care of the needy was handled locally. There was farming, lumbering, cattle, and in three directions were larger towns with industries moving into the area.

Once again in 1990, we began looking to make a change and return to a slower pace. After some time, we came to Jacksonville in 1991. We bought lands and, like so many others, we set down our roots here. It was good to see the new businesses moving in the area, the plans for some new schools, repairs of some existing schools, and street & road repairs. All this growth was needed and with more still to come. Some of the local businesses were able to grow, but too many were lost and some moved away. The last few years we have seen new industries and enterprises growing and our companies expanding, which makes others look to come here. We have fewer people moving away now, and former citizens moving back.

In retirement I have enjoyed volunteering to help others at the food pantry of my church, Our Lady of Sorrows Catholic Church. We see 400 families a month in the program. We buy our food supplies from the East Texas Food Bank at greatly discounted prices. God has blessed us with generous donors. Jacksonville is a town of many good-hearted people.

Recollections of Jacksonville

A Memoir by Bob McNiece

We are always looking for changes, but they must be done for the right reason and must be good for all. Over 230 years ago, a group of people came up with the Constitution of the United States, giving the power of governing to the people. All citizens need to support programs that support the Constitution.

The Family Auto Business

My name is William Timothy (Tim) McRae and I am a second-generation Ford dealer in Jacksonville, TX and currently represent District 3 on the City Council. I was asked to give a brief recount of my family's involvement with the Ford dealership in town and the move that led us here. I am currently 62 years old and my parents made the decision to move to Jacksonville when I was 16 years old in 1976. My father William R. (Bill) McRae was the Executive Vice-President of Moody National Bank in Galveston, TX before he and my mother, Mary McRae made the decision to move our family to Jacksonville and purchase the Ford dealership.

One of my father's accounts with the Moody Bank was the Ford dealership on the island. He floored (financed) their inventory as well as helped with the consumer financing of the automobiles when sold. Unfortunate circumstances from the death of both partners in this dealership as well as the store underperforming had led to Ford Motor Company demanding the current ownership to sell the store. The two partners that had passed away left two widows that were now the ownership of the store with no experience. The buyer Ford had found for the store was offering what would have been a substantial loss to these two ladies. My father asked the representative with Ford Motor Company if they would allow him to take over the operation of the dealership on behalf of the bank for the next 60 or 90 days (I can't remember for sure the length of time) and turn the store around into a profitable position, therefore increasing its value. Ford agreed and my father took over the day-to-day operation of the dealership.

In six weeks, he had the store operating in the black. Ford contacted the prospective buyer and informed them that Mr. McRae had the store performing profitably and if he still wanted it, he needed to contact my father and make a deal. The deal was made and after the closing took place the individual representing Ford Motor Company at the closing called my dad to the side and told him "Some of the best minds in Dearborn said that what he did here could not be done and if he ever wanted a Ford dealership to give him a call." At this time my father was about 42 years old and the thought of a career change and owning his own business was intriguing to him. He talked with my mother and they gave much thought and prayer into this consideration and made the decision to call the man with Ford Motor

Company. This began the search for the right store. Approximately two years later my father made a deal with Tommy Sullivan, the Ford dealer in Jacksonville to buy his store. He put everything on the line, and he and my mother borrowed the remainder of the money to purchase the store from First National Bank of Jacksonville, now Austin Bank, and his longtime friendship with Jeff Austin Jr. was formed.

The store at the time was franchised for Ford and Mercury, and several years later my father was granted the Lincoln franchise for Jacksonville. Since then, Mercury ceased to exist after 2011 and we sold the Lincoln franchise back to Lincoln at the end of 2021. My now partners and I came to a mutual decision with Lincoln to surrender that franchise for a monetary value agreeable to both, and in turn we were able to receive the approval needed to relocate without the additional expense required by Lincoln. Since the expected completion date of this new facility is planned by the end of 2023, I believe there is a good chance that the facility will still be the existing Ford dealership of 2072. There is no doubt my parent's decision to move our family to Jacksonville has been a very rewarding one for us. We have seen much change since 1976 and I can only imagine the changes you have seen by 2072, but I still will bet, Jacksonville is a great place to call home!

Recollections of Jacksonville

A Memoir by Tim McRae

Recollections of Jacksoville

Longhorns Come To Town and Other Memories

When Donna and I decided to get cattle, I asked my banker for advice on which type of cows we should get. He said you will lose money anyway, so get something you enjoy looking at because that is what you will mostly do. Great advice! So, Donna and I decided to get Texas Longhorns for several reasons. They are a unique breed, named after our state and bred by Mother Nature. For over 450 years, they raised themselves in the wilderness with no one feeding them. They needed to be able to take care of themselves because I knew little about cows.

The early Spanish explorers, then later, the Spanish missionaries, brought them over on sailing ships. Only the hardiest could survive. As the West was won, the Longhorn was almost bred out of existence. In 1927, the federal government formed the Wichita Wildlife Refuge in Oklahoma and stocked it with bison, elk and Texas Longhorns. There were six ranches that had preserved them. These became the foundation stock of what are now about 150 cows, bull, steers and calves. They do not feed them or pull calves. They are just turned loose on thousands of acres. Each year, in the Fall or Spring, they auction off some of the Longhorns. All of our Longhorns come from this foundation stock and each is registered. Whenever they calve, it is like an Easter egg hunt. You never know what color or color pattern they will be. Our banker was right and we've never regretted getting Texas Longhorns!

The Longhorns are something I got into in the 1980's. These are some memories from way back there. My dad said we moved "back here" in the mid 50's (I was about ten). He moved the cap pistol plant from Pasadena, Texas, in 1955. My granddad used to be a Methodist minister in the 1930's. They lived in a parsonage and he went to Lon Morris. My granddad went to Lon Morris in 1915. When we moved back, the focus was on a manufacturing location and construction. The family lived at the old Liberty Hotel. Later we rented a house on North Bolton while they built in the east side. I attended the Joe Wright Elementary School; later in 1957 I went to the Eastside Elementary School, then the old high school on Neches Street.

I remember Catfish Row where people brought their tomatoes to sell as well as other crops downtown. There were lots of trucks with produce. I remember the Ice House on the corner of Highway 69 and Highway 79 downtown. It was the coolest place to go. You put a quarter in and someone upstairs would slide a big block of ice down a chute. There used to be a railroad depot where passengers got off across from the Liberty Hotel. There was the Grandee Motel Courts and three movie theaters as well as a mission of hope. It was like a soup kitchen for hobos. They would feed them and buy a bus ticket further away. There was Tamale Joe. He made them and sold them on the street, the best tamale maker in town.

I remember playing football under head couch Bum Phillips when I was in the sixth grade. They told us we would win by the time we got to Jacksonville High School, and we did going to semi-finals twice in three years. I remember the dedication of the tomato bowl totem pole. I was the student council President, as well as co-captain of the team, and did the acceptance speech. I remember as we won, they would shut the town down (or it seemed like it) and form a caravan with city police escorting us to the next football game. We enjoyed going to the Sadler's Restaurant after the game for a chicken fried steak. All the locals were there waiting for us and would stand up and clap win or lose. I appreciate the Recollections of Jacksonville project as it means much to those of us who have been here for years as a walk down memory lane.

Recollections of Jacksonville

A Memoir by Robert Nichols

The Pink Deal

Many reputable articles have been written in years past regarding the "glory days" of the tomato industry in Jacksonville and the surrounding area. These were the days when tomatoes were picked green and brought to the packing sheds, where they were sorted and graded, wrapped in newspaper to retard ripening, packed in wooden boxes, and loaded on rail cars parked alongside railroad sidings for shipment to northern markets.

My parents and grandparents lived in those days; I didn't. By the time I took my place in the tomato patch during the 1960's, most of the packing sheds had been converted to other uses. Green tomatoes attracted little demand and brought low prices, if one could sell them at all. Yet Jacksonville still had a brisk tomato market from late May through early July each summer. These were the days of the "pink deal". What passed as "pink" tomatoes might range anywhere from "breakers" - those which revealed a faint, star-shaped blush of color on the blossom end - to those in which the color progressed from yellow near the stem end through various shades of pink and orange near the blossom end. Red tomatoes begged for buyers and brought discounted prices. Thus the term "vine-ripened", while often used in reference to Jacksonville tomatoes, was somewhat of a misnomer. The demand was for pinks and breakers, and that's what farmers brought to town. But a sharp-eyed buyer could recognize "shade-ripened" tomatoes - those picked green and allowed to color for a few days under a shade tree. These often brought a discounted price also.

In the days that I recall best, Jacksonville had what might be called a "truckers' market", at least as far as tomatoes were concerned. Packed in open-top bushel baskets, tomatoes were bid upon by buyers who operated trucks and who hauled produce to Dallas, Houston, or sometimes Austin for resale there. A few regular buyers came in from Arkansas, Oklahoma, and even as far away as Tennessee. Most of the tomatoes changed hands on the streets and vacant lots in the general vicinity of Bonner, W. Commerce, and Patton Streets. The buying and selling of tomatoes wasn't a formal auction process; it was more on the order of "I can give you $8 a bushel today." "I already been offered eight-and-a-half." "Well, alright, I guess I can go nine."

When the tomato buying deal was completed, either the buyer or the farmer would figure out a way to get their trucks alongside one another. The baskets of tomatoes would go straight from the farmer's pickup to the buyer's bobtail. A few of the local buyers, Adean Dotson and Sonny Simmons, come to mind at rented sheds where they accumulated their purchases. And then there were other local buyers, Emmett Casper, J. T. Jones, Elton Smith, and Boyd Hamilton, were some I remember being regularly present - who made smaller purchases for their roadside stands. All transactions were in cash, and it was quite eye-opening to see the fat rolls of large bills that the buyers would pull out of their pockets.

Readers may wonder if Jacksonville's truck farmers made small sales to housewives from the pickup tailgate. A few did so regularly; Uncle John Luce and Whiskers Nagel served their regular customers from their pickup beds. Ellis Reed operated an open-air produce stand under the big elm tree of knowledge that used to be on W. Commerce. We all did it on slow days, when big buyers were scarce, and we couldn't make a sale any other way. But by and large, most farmers hated what we called retailing and avoided it as much as they could. The growers much preferred to sell out as quickly as possible to a single buyer and get back to the field to get some more work done.

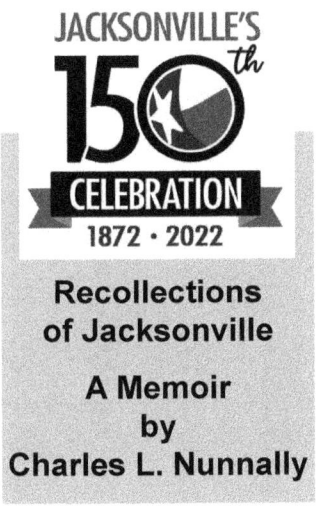

Recollections of Jacksonville

A Memoir by Charles L. Nunnally

Recollections of Jacksoville

Fifty Years Ago

In the 1970's the world was changing, but there were still things about living in a small town like Jacksonville that stayed the same. There were Friday night football games, and the Indians had a pretty good record. You could still go out to Love's Lookout and see where older generations had entertained themselves. Jacksonville was still famous as the "Tomato Capital of the World." We were also famous for being the home of Nichols Manufacturing that made the famous Nichols cap guns (this was a time when kids playing with toy guns was still okay.)

In the 1970's Jacksonville, we were experiencing an increase in manufacturing facilities due to the efforts of the city father to move away from an agricultural economy to one based on industries that were not so seasonal in nature. This change allowed the people of Jacksonville to have a steady year round income. Things were looking up in town.

In the 1970's we had the Vietnam War, Walt Disney World opened up, the Beatles broke up, the first video game "Pong" came out, the movie the Godfather came out, and President Nixon resigned. All these events were happening, but Jacksonville pretty much rolled with the flow. You have to remember that there was no internet or social media, so people couldn't get stirred up as easily as they do today.

Based on today's world, I am pretty sure that in 2072 America will not be the same as it was in the 1970's or even today. People will have forgotten that the founding fathers wanted to establish a country where everyone had equal opportunities, not equal incomes. If I had a goal for the people of 2072, it would be that if you have not somehow gotten as close to the vision of the country's founders as possible, that you should somehow strive to get there. They had a good plan, but greed and separation from God corrupted it. Good luck and may peace be with you.

Joe Peacock spent his life in Jacksonville, and was a business man who owned the Peacock Basket Factory,, the Peacock Plastics Company, and the Peacock Marketing Company. He was a dedicated member of the Our Lady of Sorrows Catholic Church.

Recollections of Jacksoville

A Nurse's Tale

My medical journey in Jacksonville began in late 1973 upon moving here with my husband Jimmie who had been hired by Lon Morris College. Once our two children, Beth and Matt, were enrolled in school, I accepted a position as the 3-11 nursing supervisor at the Nan Travis Hospital. Several years later, I moved to the Nan Travis Clinic on the loop as the supervisor of the LVN staff. Within a few years Dr. William Milawski was hired and sent to set up a clinic in Alto. I was offered the position as his office nurse, which I accepted. We worked together for the next ten years. One interesting event I remember was when Dr. Milawski and I were making a house call on our lunch hour. This was before cars had GPS devices, and the instructions we were given was to look for a cup towel the home owner would hang on their front porch.

In 1990 I accepted a position as a JISD school nurse and remained there for thirteen years. A highlight of my early time at the high school was establishing a clinic in the high school. Prior to one being built, students had to lie on palates on the floor in the principal's office. Upon retiring, I spent about six years working at Project HOPE promoting healthy life style information, community health screening, and participated in other community activities.

Reflecting on those early years has clearly shown the progress made in our medical arena. Sadly the Travis Clinic did not survive, however; our community has two major hospitals and a new HOPE clinic along numerous other clinics and our health department. I am especially thrilled with the HOPE clinic with which I worked in partnership in its beginning. HOPE Clinic is dedication to caring for the uninsured in our County and is in partnership with college nursing students who, as part of their training, are becoming a new generation of educated health providers for our rural communities. I am confident medical progress will continue in Jacksonville, and honored to have worked with so many talented, dedicated people. I am still enjoying the blessings of their friendship and love.

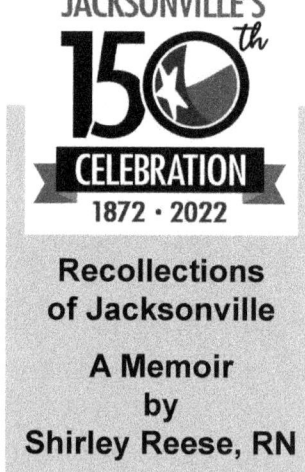

Recollections of Jacksonville

A Memoir by Shirley Reese, RN

The Tomato Symbols

Jacksonville is known for tomatoes, Tomato Fest and the Tomato Bowl. What addition could be added and be unique? BIG 665 lb. concrete tomatoes! Randy Gorham, formerly Jacksonville Chamber of Commerce Treasurer in 2010 created the idea of having specialty concrete tomatoes to be placed in front of businesses or homes, just everywhere.

I contacted a company in south Texas that had been known to make other specialty items to see if we can challenge his talent for a big tomato. It was a challenge but one, David, with Double D Statuary, was willing to create something new for Jacksonville. Several models were created until the perfect one was approved. There is a plastic bucket located inside the concrete as if not, the tomato would weigh almost 1,000 lbs.

How were the tomatoes going to be moved and delivered? David, with Double D, created a special sling that could be used by a forklift. Now, I had to find someone willing to store and deliver the concrete tomatoes. So many unknowns as I had no idea how many the Chamber would sell or how long this project will last. This, also, included a company willing to unload when shipment arrives. I visited with Teresa Langley, Harry's Building Materials, sharing our excitement of this new project, but we help with delivery and a place to store the tomatoes. Immediately, Harry's Building Materials jumped on the 'tomato project' to deliver the 665 lb. tomatoes.

Again, I didn't know what to share with those willing to help as I had no clue about the life of this project, I've didn't know if the special strap would work and if the tomatoes would sell. Now, where can the tomatoes be delivered, especially the first delivery? GME, on the Loop jumped on this opportunity for the first load of delivery, which took approximately 10 months. See, with one mold, only one tomato could be poured a day and then there was the issue about the transportation of how many could be delivered to Jacksonville from south Texas.

We continued to move forward learning new challenges, but determined. Now, is the time to market the tomatoes, hoping the sale of the concrete tomatoes would sell. Oh, the 665 lb. tomatoes were and still a hit! Businesses, individuals and churches wanted to be the first to have a tomato. Everyone was talking tomatoes and how to decorate their tomato. Judy

Seamands, Wall Works by Judy, along with a couple of individuals painted tomatoes. Announcement of the first shipment arriving involved working with the Double D Statuary, trucking company, GME, and Harry's Building Materials to coordinate the date and time.

In early, February 2012, Chamber Board members, individuals, and the media were all at GME for the first shipment of tomatoes. Harry's Building Materials had the perfect equipment for delivery. The first shipment of tomatoes was SOLD and more orders were placed as we had 75 orders on a waiting list. It took over 8 months to finally catch up on the orders. The first year, we sold 75. Harry's Building Materials stored and managed delivery for ALL the tomatoes, working closely with the Chamber. After several years, the Jacksonville Chamber Board of Directors wanted to continue the excitement and offer a smaller tomato. Another new smaller mold was made and the weight of the smaller tomato is 175 lbs. Another shipment of large and smaller tomatoes was delivered and again all sold.

The larger tomato is the BIGGEST hit as the Chamber has calls regularly to tell the story of the concrete tomato. There is a tinman tomato, ice cream tomato, hamburger tomato, billboard tomato, basket of tomatoes, Indian tomato, and so many others. Scavenger hunts have taken place during Tomato Fest and many other times to find the specialty tomatoes here in town. Now, there are tomatoes in Ding Dong, Texas, Warren, Arkansas, West Texas, and Houston. Bolton Park located on El Paso and South Jackson is the home to many graduating classes' tomatoes. When we think we have sold the last one, then we have another order. In 2021, the tomato mold was broken, and a discussion was made of do we invest in another mold, will we sell more tomatoes, and whether if Harry's Building Materials wants to continue the delivery and storage? The answers were all YES! In late, 2021, the Jacksonville Chamber announced another order will be available in early 2022. Will the 665 lb. tomato end? I think not!

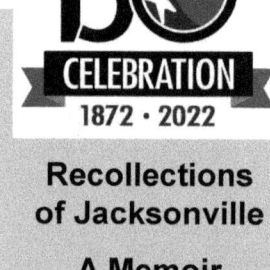

Recollections of Jacksonville

A Memoir by Peggy Renfro

We've Come A Long Way

I was born in the community of "Low Baptist" to Wesley "Son" Robinson and Pearline Clemons Robinson. I attended elementary school in the Pine Grove community before transferring to the Fred Douglas School in Jacksonville. At an early age I grew up doing farming chores with my family. In the fall we would go out west to pick cotton to help with living expenses. I would have to milk cows before going to school, and walk to catch the school bus. My father grew vegetables for the family. We had chickens and I drew water from a well. On Saturday the family would come into the city where I attended the movies a lot before returning home. My father and mother didn't finish school. My father had to work to support the family.

I attended and received a certificate in Business Administration from the Tyler Commercial College. I attended Jacksonville Baptist College after graduating from Fred Douglas High School. Then I began to plant my roots in life. In 1966 I married the love of my life, Doris Calvin from Jacksonville, and have celebrated 56 years together. We have three children and six grandchildren. I'm a faithful member of the Sweet Union Baptist Church, where I have served as chairman of the trustees, treasurer of the brotherhood, member of the budget committee, and member of the joint board.

I worked as a sales assistant for Sears for 17 years before taking my current position at the Sweet Union apartments for the last 31 years. At my job, people say what me is on their minds to keeps in touch with what our community needs. I have also worked for 30 years in the JISD Transportation Department. I see a lot of people in my work and they are never shy about telling me what city issues concern them.

I have served on the Jacksonville City Council since 2003, and served as mayor pro-tem for three years. I had served on the city adjustment and rehabilitation boards before being elected to the city council. I have served on the Board of Directors of the Travis Towers. I had to act as the mayor from October 2014 to June 2014 after the death of Mayor Kenneth Melvin. These jobs have been exciting and rewarding challenges. After all, we are put on this earth to serve. I was instrumental in securing the play ground at the Lincoln Park, as well as the provisions for building a bridge across the walkway and installing lights in the park. Even though my responsibility as a councilman is policy making, I help with water bill problems, personnel problems, and help people of color get employment. I'm a man of few words, but I don't mind speaking up for others.

Jacksonville has certainly changed a lot since I grew up. The city is growing and it's getting better. I have seen some major projects and business come to fruition. I am happy to be part of this growth. Since being on the city council, we have been able to freeze the tax rates. We have just completed the new police and fire station in the City Safety Center. We have a new water meter system where leaks are detected and your meter can be turned and read from the Public Works office. Our Police Department has more diversity in the work force. We have people of color in leadership and management positions within the city. New business is coming to town. We have three new schools and our academic record is great. This is a long way from where I started.

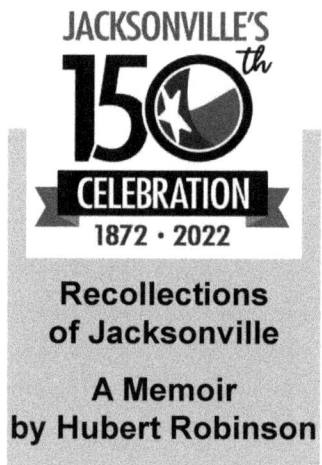

JACKSONVILLE'S 150th CELEBRATION 1872 · 2022

Recollections of Jacksonville

A Memoir by Hubert Robinson

My Personal Memories

Hello, My name is Nancy Sonntag, and if you are reading this memoir, you probably have a connection, interest, or both concerning the Sesquicentennial of Jacksonville, Texas. This includes the history and people involved in the recollections included in this book.

I am a native Texan, but I did not plant my roots in Jacksonville until August of 1986. My husband Fred began working with his brother-in-law, Bill McRae, at Bill McRae Ford in Jacksonville. I started teaching at the old Joe Wright Elementary which was located on Kickapoo Street at that time. I was fortunate to begin my Jacksonville teaching career under the leadership of Principal Gene Tankersley, and I taught with many outstanding teachers including Joyce Folden, Peggy Harton, and many more quality teachers. My children began attending Jacksonville Middle School and Jacksonville High School. I wish to add that my children received very strong educational backgrounds which prepared them to become successful college graduates. Hats off to Ann Chandler for giving my children the background to write those pesky, but necessary, college essays and research papers.

In 1996, I made a change in schools within the district and I became the Language Arts teacher at the newly established Compass Center. Doctor Leslie George was the principal and John Mark Lester was the assistant principal. This career move presented many excellent experiences and challenges as well. The dedicated staff at the Compass Center succeeded in keeping a number of at-risk students in school until they obtain their high school diplomas. Excellent staff there as well.

In June of 2003, I resigned my position as English teacher at the Compass Center. I took an early retirement to be in the Dallas area with my brother who was receiving treatments for cancer at that time. Sadly, he lost the battle in February of 2004.

Not ready for complete retirement, I took two positions. The first position was teaching Developmental Reading and Writing at Jacksonville College. Dr. Edwin Crank was president of Jacksonville College at that time. I was privileged to work with International students as well as local students. Learning about the different customs from the International students was an added bonus, I was fortunate to work with a quality staff there, and I began friends with many on the faculty of Jacksonville College. Later, the Jacksonville Literacy Council became more involved with Jacksonville College when our organization began holding our GED classes on their campus. This relationship began under the leadership of Dr. Edwin Crank, and it continued to flourish when Dr. Crank retired, and Dr. Mike Smith became the president.

The other position was Program Director for the Jacksonville Literacy Council. I am still working in this extremely rewarding capacity. Here is a brief explanation of how the Jacksonville Literacy Council was established. It began in 1992 with a survey titled "Goals for Jacksonville". This survey was provided to the citizens of Jacksonville, and all of Cherokee County. The purpose of the survey was to determine the needs of the residents of the area, and how to improve the quality of life for all residents in the area. One of the needs identified was the high illiteracy rate in and around the Jacksonville area. Thus, the Jacksonville Literacy Council was formed. Persons instrumental in establishing the Jacksonville Literacy Council were Dr. Edwin Crank, present mayor of Jacksonville Randy Gorham, Barbara Gregg, Jim Lord, Mary Brown, and Jeff Austin Jr. as well as other dedicated individuals.

The Jacksonville Literacy Council offers services including basic literacy, GED and E.S.L., and Citizenship preparation. The Council was active for a number of years, and then, due to several reasons, became inactive.

When I became the Program Director in January 2004, our operating budget was quite limited. The Jacksonville United Fund, Rotary Club, Kiwanis Club, and the Friends of the Jacksonville Library, as well as individual donations, helped keep our organization in the position to continue our efforts. We also hosted a Corporate Spelling Bee every year in May as a fundraiser. Due to the COVID pandemic, our organization has not been able to host this event for two years, but we hope to be able to have it again in May 2022.

Meanwhile, back to finances. I was asked to speak at a Library Board meeting in 2007. A gentleman in attendance, Dr. Sam Hopkins, took an interest in our worthy cause. He was asked to attend a meeting with the

Board of Directors of the Jacksonville Literacy Council. He soon became the President of the Board. If any of you have had the pleasure of working with Sam, you know he is a real go-getter who makes things happen. He got our board in strong shape and he implemented many ambitious goals and events for the Jacksonville Literacy Council. We are still an active organization and a valuable asset to our community. Many thanks to Sam for his leadership.

In summation, I have enjoyed the wonderful people of Jacksonville, and I am proud to have been a part of its history. My thanks go to Sam Hopkins for providing me with the opportunity to contribute to this book.

From Centennial to Sesquicentennial

From where I sit today, our sweet Jacksonville has been an adventure and a joy. Back in 1972, when we celebrated the 100th birthday of our town, it was an amazing spectacle to an 11 year old. Our teachers, grandparents, even us kids dressed in period garb. There were contests, flags and a book published. We had a parade up Jackson Street and a "Spectacular Production" in the Tomato Bowl. One of the coolest things was the Time Capsule, buried at the corner of City Park. This year, on May 11th, we're going to dig it up!

Growing up, my bicycle carried me anywhere I wanted to go. There were lots of shops downtown and fun stuff to explore and discover. We got to learn of fires when the now silent tower that sits behind the feedstore downtown blared the signal. Jacksonville was also serenaded by church bells ringing and everybody could tell which way the ambulance was heading. Today, you can still hear the Basket Factory whistle, that hasn't changed.

As a grandmother, Jacksonville continues to amaze me. There are new faces and new places and our blessed lifestyle in God's country appeals to more and more new neighbors. New arrivals we meet tell us that they love how friendly our town is. That's something that probably hasn't changed...our town has been a great place to live since 1872, I know that hasn't changed since 1972 and I wouldn't expect it to change before 2072.

Now, in 2022, the date has arrived for us to throw a Sesquicentennial birthday celebration for our sweet 75766. It is time to come home, come together and come downtown to celebrate on October 22, 2022. Plans are evolving, but we'll need everyone's help to spread the word. Tell your family now; plan a trip home for the celebration! Make plans to gather up friends and participate. We're going to have a great time and maybe, just maybe, we can all get together and amaze some present day 11 year olds.

Recollections of Jacksonville

A Memoir by Kathleen Stanfill

Jacksonville's History of Golf, Nearly 100 Years

When spring time rolls around and the flowers start blooming, my thoughts turn to the golf season and especially the Masters tournament. I was first exposed to the game of golf in the spring of 1964 when I began taking golf lessons from Mr. Murray Toland.

Mr. Toland started giving free golf lessons, at the Cherokee Country Club to Jacksonville's aspiring young golfers in the 1940s, and continued helping young golfers for over 50 years. One of my favorite memories of Mr. Toland's golf lessons was the season ending putting contest and hamburger supper followed by a 1-hour video of the previous year's Masters Golf tournament.

Jacksonville is very fortunate to have one of the best, small town golf courses in East Texas. The Cherokee Golf Ranch, formerly known as Cherokee Country Club, opened in 1936 as a 9-hole golf course, and was extended to 18 holes in the mid to late 1970s.

Although Cherokee Country Club was founded in 1936 it was not Jacksonville's first golf course. That distinction belongs to the Jacksonville Golf Course which opened in 1926 near what is now the Hillcrest housing addition on the city's east side. It was a 9-hole course with oil and sand greens. Prior to the invention of the wooden tee, golfers made tees out of sand. The Jacksonville Golf Course supplied golfers with a box of wet sand from which golfers would fashion a raised mound using either their hands or a cone-shaped mold. After a golfer hit the ball on the green, they had to smooth out the area between the ball and the hole with an instrument called a drag. Unlike today, the cup stayed in the middle of the green and was not moved around the green each day.

Recollections of Jacksonville

A Memoir by Dick Stone

Recently the Jacksonville Economic Development Corporation acquired the Cherokee Golf Ranch, ensuring Jacksonville's rich golf history will continue for many years to come.

Remembering the Crosbys

The Crosby Furniture was a constant in Jacksonville for over 40 years. It was owned by J.O. and June Crosby and began its operation in 1960. June Crosby was raised in Jacksonville, and after attending college, she married J.O. Crosby, and shortly thereafter, they moved to Jacksonville in 1954 to establish their permanent residence. The Crosbys were married for 70 years and lived in the same home that they purchased in 1954.

The Crosbys had three girls, who all helped in various ways in the furniture store. J.O. and June purchased the furniture store from R.H. and Dezzie Chesnut, June's parents. The Crosby Furniture store was located in the 100 block of Woodrow Street and consisted of three separate buildings in that block. The Liberty Hotel was a Jacksonville landmark and was located next door to Crosby furniture. In the height of its popularity, the Liberty Hotel was considered "the place" to have Jacksonville functions. It also was packed with buyers from all the country during tomato season. It was truly a devastating event when the Liberty Hotel burned to the ground in March, 1972.

The Crosby Furniture was in business for over 40 years at the same location. Everyone in Jacksonville knew that the Crosbys loved playing golf, with J.O. and June being routinely spotted on the golf course after work. While actively involved in the furniture store, J.O. and June started another business that involved their love for golf. J & R Golf Club Company began operations in 1970 and was a golf club manufacturing and repair facility. This business proved to be a successful career choice for the Crosbys, with their selection as the Ben Hogan Repair Center for East Texas, and a list of more than 600 country clubs all over the country as their customers.

As their children grew and their interests became more diversified, Crosby Furniture began to re-allocate their space in the three buildings. First, J & R Golf took over one of the buildings. Nancy and Janice Crosby began twirling competitively, with the furniture store once again dedicating another one of its buildings for use by the "Crosby Twirling Studio". This twirling studio was attended by the majority of young girls in Jacksonville. Both Nancy and Janice were the instructors for the Studio and could be seen after school each day working with their students in learning how to twirl.

The middle building remained the hub of the Crosby's businesses and would be the place where friends, family, and customers would come to visit, talk about golf, furniture, twirling, and anything else that was the topic for the day. June Crosby was an accomplished artist and golfer and was instrumental in starting the Jacksonville Art League and the Ladies Golf Association. The Crosbys were always actively involved in Jacksonville activities. J.O. Crosby passed away at the age of 94 in 2020. June Crosby, at the age of 91, still lives in the same house that she and J.O. bought in 1954, and she remains an avid fan of the game of golf. In fact, she is still being asked to help teach new golfers in Jacksonville.

How Texas Basket Factory Got Its Name

We are really proud of our Texas Heritage. My great-great-great-great-grandfather came to Texas before the Texas revolution with Stephen F. Austin. And his son William Physicks Zuber was the last living survivor of the Battle of San Jacinto.

In the mid 1970's, my wife Jackie Ballard Swanson and I purchased what was then named Newton-Shank Manufacturing Company. We changed the name to the Texas Basket Company which we operated for almost 50 years. We were also able to celebrate the 100th anniversary of this business in 2019. We grew and diversified the business which became one of only a few basket factories left in the United States. Jackie created a retail factory gift store at our business which quickly became a local tourist attraction and destination point. This brought a lot of people to Jacksonville.

Our children attended the Jacksonville school system. Our daughter Shannon was a captain of the drill team and homecoming queen (as was her mother when she attended JHS). She later became a Tyler Junior College Apache Bell for two years. Shannon was the first Miss Tyler USA to be crowned and went on to represent Tyler in the Miss Texas USA pageant. She was also a Dallas Cowboys Cheerleader for 5 years and was able to cheer at Super Bowl XXX which the Cowboys won. She was chosen to represent the Dallas Cowboys Cheerleaders in the 2003 Pro Bow in Hawaii which is a great honor.

Our son Moon Swanson created and developed the 1836 Chuckwagon Race which became a local, western event attracting several thousand people to our ranch in Neches, Texas each year. Moon also developed and raised a line of quarter horses using the King bloodline. The horses are descendants of King P-234 and several have done well in the Cowboy Mounted Shooting events in the United States. The horses and Moon himself have done well nationally in this newer equestrian sport.

I was also very fortunate to be associated with two other Jacksonville residents, Pat McCown and Bobby Redd, to participate in basketball Senior Olympics for 10+ years. We actually won a National Gold Medal in the 2016 games. Living in a small town has been an enjoyable and rewarding experience. We hope that the newer generation to come will recognize the small town benefits and continue to keep Jacksonville a good place to live, raise a family and thrive.

Rodeo Sesquicentennial Memories

The Jacksonville Rodeo Association was less than 10 years old when the Jacksonville Centennial was celebrated. It recently marked the 61th annual event. In the fall of 1962 the idea of "bigtime rodeo with entertainers" was born and plans were rapidly made for the first show in July of 1963. Much work had to be done such as building an arena, hiring stock producers, music people, entertainers and lots of other jobs.

All of these jobs fell to volunteers from the Jacksonville Riders Club and the Jacksonville Lions Club. When the Rodeo Association was formed, it drew 12 directors from each club to make decisions for the association. By July of 1963 all was in place and Michael Landon of the television show "Bonanza" was hired to entertain all four nights. He turned out to be the most popular star ever. Landon died just prior to the rodeo one year and the association, the only time ever, presented a $1,000 scholarship to a high school graduate, in his memory.

So many entertainers came to the rodeo. Jacksonville's own Neal McCoy entertained three times, as did Jon and Jim Haggar from Hee Haw Show. Several others came twice. Stars included were Rex Allen and his horse Koko, Eddy Arnold, Clu Gulager, Peter Breck, Ken Curtis, Jerry Lee Lewis, Carl Smith, Don Cherry, Tommy Overstreet, and Red Steagall.

The Oak Ridge Boys were so popular both on and off the stage. Joe Bonsai, tenor for the group, was a heart throb for the girls who nick-named him "Smiley". The group and their band came to town in an old tour bus and every time they started to leave the arena or the hotel someone with a strong battery had to "jump the engine" to get it going. They were a happy bunch and a real crowd pleaser. Shortly after their local performance, their recording "Ya'll Comeback Saloon", reached number one status and the rest is history.

Other stars were Joe Stampley, Moe Bandy, Johnny Rodriguez and Lee Greenwood, who introduced what would become his signature song, "God Bless the USA". Greenwood returned the next year and closed his show with a magnificent performance of his song. Arena lights were off, only a spotlight trained on a very spirited black horse circling the arena with its rider holding the American flag as Greenwood sang "God Bless the USA." It truly was a beautiful sight.

Other stars included Steve Wariner, Gene Watson, Eddy Raven, Mason Dixon, Mel McDaniel, John Schneider, Keith Whitley, T. Graham Brown, Billy Joe Royal, Asleep at the Wheel, Lynn Anderson, T.G. Sheppard, The Noblemen, Charly McClain and Wayne Massey. Garth Brooks, new to entertainment, entertained a sold-out crowd, as did Brooks & Dunn. More stars were Jo-El Sonnier, Gary Stewart, Lionel Cartwright, Doug Stone, Sammy Kershaw, Janie Frickie, McBride and the Ride, Aaron Tippin, Shenandoah, Doug Supernaw, Boy Howdy, Rick Trevino, Woody Lee and George Ducas.

More stars were Wade Hayes, David Lee Murphy, Chely Wright, David Kersh, Ty England, David Allen Coe, James Bona my, Lee Ann Womack, John Conlee, Jerry Jeff Walker, Kenny Chesney, Rhett Adkins Chad Brock, Mark Wills, Perfect Stranger, Dianna Littlepage, Kentucky Headhunters, John Anderson, Ricky Lynn Gregg, Los Rivales, Blake Shelton, Tommy Shane Stiener, Starskey & Johnson, Billy Currington, Brooks Atwood, Pat Green, Chris Cagle, Stoney Larue, Randy Rogers Band, Branded Duo, Zona Jones, Larry Mahan, and several others.

Several young women from the area were honored as Rodeo Queen including Phyllis Darby, Bitsy Goforth, Jane Tipton, Fancy Shank, Frances Stover, Jan Woolery, Doty Phillips, Cathy Bolton, Mary Beth McGee, Tracey Holcombe and others.

The 16th rodeo featured a new format with the forming of the Western Week Committee. This group planned activities for every day of the week, starting with the ever popular Monday night street dance in the downtown area, and continuing with a dog show, children's activities, parade, chuck wagon lunch and much more. The rodeo has provided entertainment, fun and excitement through the years and has seen many changes in the way it operates and the people who make it possible. Funds from the event have been used for educational and charitable endeavors in the community through Lions Club,

Recollections of Jacksoville

Riders Club, Career Women's Civic Club, Jaycees, Project Graduation and numerous other organizations.

Several directors of the rodeo board have been awarded the John Justice Standard of the West award for their outstanding volunteer work. At least ten directors have been recognized by the Jacksonville Chamber of Commerce as Outstanding Citizen of the Year. Byron Underwood has served as president for several years and the Cowboy churches have had a great hand in its production for several years.

The Hometown Newspaper

Just before Jacksonville celebrated its centennial in 1972, the Jacksonville Daily Progress had built a new facility across the street from the Tomato Bowl. The old letter-press at the corner of Main and E. Rusk St. was replaced with a new off-set printing press. Everything was new, clean and bright. As plans for the centennial celebration were announced, Progress then-owner B.H. Broiles announced that he wanted a 100-page centennial edition. Plans were laid, the staff got busy, and they exceeded the order. There were sections on churches, education, business, industry, clubs, sports and other interests. With 30 employees, there was much work, cooperation, and satisfaction with that endeavor. The centennial celebration spanned the whole week, culminating with a spectacular pageant in the Tomato Bowl on Saturday night, featuring dozens of local residents. The newspaper stayed open that night "So that those who wished could cross the street and visit the new facility." It was so exciting. During the next 50 years the paper has continued to cover Jacksonville events and serve advertisers and persons needing job printing. People throughout town wore period clothing during the centennial celebration, including women who worked at the newspaper.

I worked at the JDP from 1962 until 1995. It was a marvelous education. In about 1969, when I moved from teletype setting and clerical work to editorial, I started covering Jacksonville High School. That soon spread to other campuses, and all were rewarding. We had a marvelous "lifestyle" section on Sunday. Most Saturday nights people were sitting in the parking lot waiting for the paper to come off the press. Although I worked six days a week and covered lots of night events, I loved my job. I worked under four publishers and three editors. I learned a lot from all of them, particularly Mr. and Mrs. Broiles and Maris Fletcher. Don Wallace and Steve Lee were outstanding sports editors. When Mrs. Broiles retired as Society editor, she relinquished her job to me. Through the years literally hundreds of pictures and stories told of weddings, teas, coffees, school events, births, deaths, family and class reunions, anniversaries and you name it! It was all about local folks. In 1980 I started the weekly column "Personality." That was such an enjoyable part of my work for 15 years as I met, interviewed and wrote about 750 unforgettable people.

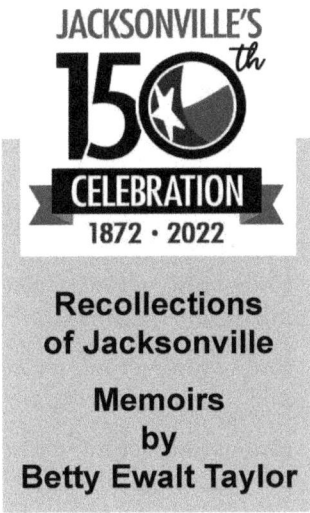

Recollections of Jacksoville

A Jacksonville Child's Memory of WW-II

My memories of WW-II are few but vivid, for I was young, and I realize now- as an octogenarian- how much that era marked and shaped me. My WW-I veteran father, Clarence John Taylor, was rarely living with us during that period, as he worked at various war plants throughout the South, including the Atomic Bomb Plant at Oak Ridge, Tennessee, and an artillery factory outside of Borger, Texas. Mostly, my mom and I lived in Jacksonville, Texas, my birthplace then and my retirement home now.

I recall not so much the big events of wartime Jacksonville, but rather the small things, things a child would notice. I understood my Uncle Bill Holcomb was a B-17 pilot in the war, but did not grasp that he was in England with the 8th Air Force. I knew we did not have a car and walked most places with Mom hoisting me up on her shoulders when I was tired as we hiked from our small house on Ft. Worth Street to Aunt Reba and Uncle John Tom Ahearn's place on San Antonio Street. Even if we had a car, there were no tires available due to war-time rubber shortages. Dad drove a 1941 Plymouth, but he lived far away from us, so we walked.

Home activities are particularly clear. Tin cans were collected, cleaned and squashed as a mother-son project all in preparation for the scheduled Boy Scout pick up. Mom said we were helping the war effort because those tin cans were to be converted to bullets and tanks to defeat America's enemies. I assisted in other ways too. At meal time the phrase "Have a victory plate" was repeated regularly. In short, eat all your food, waste not, for that small accomplishment was a step toward victory. I raised my two sons, Mike and Chris, using that very line to encourage them to finish their food. I have often wondered if other people used the phrase.

Of course, we attempted a Victory Garden as well, but I only remember eating one lone carrot and perhaps a radish as Mom was not much of a gardener. Our heart, however, was in the right place on the issue.

Regarding food, one additional thing sticks out. Butter was rationed (I still have the family ration books that Mom had kept under her bed until her death). So margarine was invented as a substitute, but it was white and did not have the butter appearance. A packet of yellow food dye was combined with the margarine, and I helped Mom stir it all together until the color was acceptable.

Sometimes children draw wrong conclusions based on what they see and hear. In the home of my grandparents, Jess and Lois Holcomb, on Bryan Street, there was a framed picture in their bedroom of General Douglas McArthur. Since every framed photo in the house was a relative, I assumed that the general was my uncle! And that is what I told people! Even after I learned different, Douglas McArthur remained an important figure for me as I grew up; after all he was once my uncle for a few years.

Vividly I recall military uniforms, especially on trains. I think Mom and I were on the way someplace to visit Dad, and the train was packed by solders. Often, they took me off my mom's hands by offering to walk me up and down the aisles. It was a GI on the train who gave me my first piece of Double Bubble chewing gum, another casualty of war time shortages. I usually asked them if they knew my Uncle Bill. Keeping me happy, they said they did, and that made me feel good.

But things were not always good. On December 9, 1943, Uncle Bill's B-17 crashed flying out of an airfield in Bovingdon, England. All ten men aboard were killed. Mother was in the kitchen with Aunt Louise Stripling when she got the call from her older brother, JH Holcomb. Later I saw the Gold Star on my grandmother's window and was told what that meant. Many tears were shed and would continue over the years.

Recollections of Jacksonville

Memoirs by John H. Taylor

My last firm recollection from the war was on Wednesday, August 15, 1945. I heard a loud whistle blow from the Jacksonville city tower announcing V-J Day (Victory over Japan). The war was over, but the memories remained.

True Blue and Gold

As I reflect back on my 72 years in Jacksonville, Texas, I think of all the people who have made me what I am today. From the pillars in our community, to the guidance from those in my Church, and to the wonderful people from JISD who raised me, nurtured me, and worked beside me, what a great 72 years it has been.

From working at Corbett Bivins little grocery store by the Tomato Bowl for 50 cents an hour, to walking across street to get an ice cream cone from J. N. Grimes at Dairy Queen, cheering and twirling at the Tomato Bowl, Chapel Choir trips with Venson Roberts with Central Baptist Church, eating at old Sadlers restaurant which later became The Hut and we danced there, all are precious memories.

Bealls General Offices and Warehouse were where my mom and dad worked. The Bealls' family was our family. Everyone took care of each other.

I married at 18 to Sandy Terry, a Jacksonville boy too!! We did live 5 years at Lake Jackson before moving back for Sandy to teach here. I went back to school and began my teaching career with JISD in 1978. Things were different back then. I graduated as well as another high school teacher's wife. I got a call from superintendents Secretary saying they were so excited I was graduating and they needed me to teach reading at East Side School. This other wife got a call to teach math at West Side School. We called each other as I was a math teacher and she was a reading teacher. I called the superintendent's Secretary and said I was so excited but my degree was math and the other lady was reading. Secretary said, "oh great, y'all just switch." So I started at West Side school with Jimmy Sanford as my first boss. He was tough. Taught me so many good work habit. He was the best! I had taught about 10 years and got a call one day from Central Office. They were being audited and I had never completed an application for a job and I needed to do that and I needed to write my philosophy of education. Times have changed!!!Lots if paperwork has to be done today!

I continued to teach and go back to school. Was a teacher, assistant principal, principal, curriculum director, and assistant superintendent. The people along the way are the joys of living in Jacksonville! I am watching my former students' kids play sports!! I was at a tournament out of town the other day, a coach I knew from another town said why are you here. Told him the coach was my son's best friend growing up, the team was my former students' children. About that time one if the dads came by to hug my neck! My blood is blue and gold!!

Last month I heard a former student calling my name in an airport in a Houston!! Last week at an out if town game, former student came to sit with me during half time! On Facebook a former student sent me pictures of his daughters this week! The joys of being in education in a town the size of Jacksonville! I was honored as the second Influential Indian by my co workers! Now as a member if the Jacksonville Education Board, I work to see our community give back to the teachers and students through scholarships and teacher grants.

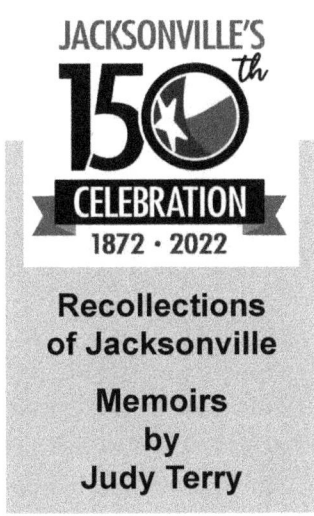

Recollections of Jacksonville

Memoirs by Judy Terry

The Tilley Family and the Coca-Cola Bottling Company

I've been asked to write about the Coca-Cola bottling company in Jacksonville. To do justice to the story about the family business, I must first begin with my great-grandfather, George Tilley. He was born in 1848 and was a merchant in "old" Jacksonville and operated a saloon too. When the railroad arrived in 1872, it missed the town by several miles and merchants quickly moved to the new town site. George Tilley was one of those who moved their business on ox-drawn wagons. It is reported he "put up" the first business in the new town of Jacksonville, which was a saloon.

My grandfather, Harry Park "Pat" Tilley, was a pharmacist in the Ambrose Johnson Drug Store in "new" Jacksonville. In the back of the drug store was the Crown Bottling Works--a soft drink manufacturing facility which my grandfather purchased from Ambrose. It was located on Commerce Street.

In October 1904, "Pat" obtained a franchise for Coca-Cola, and in 1908 moved the business to 224 South Bolton Street. This building was among the first in Jacksonville to have a concrete floor, which gave better support for the machinery. Coca-Cola was added to the drinks already being sold such as orange, grape, root beer and sarsaparilla. All drinks were sold May through September, the warmer months of the year. The bottling process was interesting. Bottles were filled and a stopper inserted in the opening and the bottles stored in wooden crates upside down. This ensured proper pressure of CO_2 in the bottles and kept it sealed. When you wanted to drink the soda water, you pressed the bottle under the edge of a table or against a firm surface and the stopper went down into the bottle. And as it did, it made a "pop" sound. Hence the name soda pop. You drank the soda with the stopper down in the bottle.

Because roads were in poor condition at the time, the viability of the Coca-Cola franchise depended upon the railroads that ran through Jacksonville. Coca-Cola was shipped to customers Flint, Gresham, and all points in-between.

During the 1930's when I visited the plant, accompanied by my mother, I also visited businesses that occupied the space next to the plant. One was a lock and key shop owned by Gene Cox, and another was Andrew's Feed Store. Mother is an amazing story in her own right. Mable Maud Clark was a secretary at the Fleischmann Yeast office in Dallas when she met my father. Their offices were in the same building. He ran the Electrified Water Company, which my grandfather owned. The process was used in our plant till the city drilled the first water well in Jacksonville.

In July 1937, my grandfather "Pat" and my father, Gordon Tilley, moved the facility to the last location it would occupy, Main and Nacogdoches. This location is now a parking lot for U.T. East Texas Medical. After the move, products included, of course, Coca-Cola which was in a 6 ½ oz. bottle. The soda waters were in a 7 oz. bottle and the bottle had Tilley embossed on the side and Jacksonville on the bottom. Over time the soda water bottles would change shape and capacity.

My family lived on Lloyd Avenue. While the new plant was being built, I rode my tricycle up to the corner of Nacogdoches to watch them. The building was made of a special brick in red and black colors. To make the second floor, a ramp was constructed so brick and mortar could be pushed up the ramp in wheel barrows to the brick layers who worked off wooden scaffolding.

A big change occurred December 7, 1941, when Pearl Harbor was attacked. Sugar, an essential part of the Coca-Cola syrup, became a restricted product. We were rationed each month, and our ration was based on previous years' purchases of syrup. We got more syrup during the summer months because we sold more Coke in summer than other months. We also had to ration Coca-Cola sales to our customers.

I went to work for my father at about 12 years of age. I got paid 12 ½ cents an hour, up to $1 a day; that was a lot of money for a 12 year old! Also, during the war years my Dad went to school cafeterias and got their empty gallon metal cans that fruits and vegetables came in. He cut the cans into strips and made the crowns (caps) for the bottling operation. Metal was difficult to come by because it was needed for the military.

The WW-II ended in 1945, and in the early 1950s changes were made in the Coke industry. We saw the introduction of a 10 oz. Coke bottle and the 12 oz. cans. The first cans my Dad bought were a 48 can case, double the size of the other soft drink bottlers. It met some resistance because of the cost which was twice that of our competitors, but it did have twice the cans. In 1951, it was off to Texas A&M for me. In the summer it was expected I would work at the Coke plant, usually driving an extra truck and delivering Cokes to customers. My route was the City of Alto and surrounding areas.

After graduation from A&M, I worked at the plant till October1st, and then it was off to join the US Army. Two years later I returned and worked at the Coke plant. My Dad announced that I was coming back and would be the Sales Manager. Little did I know it, but I took a pay cut to come back to civilian life. I had a lot to learn, and did so by jumping in and just doing whatever was needed. I drove a delivery truck and worked on the production line. I learned to fix vending machines by riding along with my Uncle John; that was valuable. When he died, suddenly I became the mechanic on both the open type cooler and vending machines.

From about 1960 until 1969, I worked closely with my Dad. On November 6, 1969, I got a call from the hospital, my father who had been ill, and passed away. Talk about a change in life, I went from going from being one of the guys to being the boss. Fortunately, everyone at the plant seemed like family, and were very supported of me. Time marched on, and with time came changes to the soft drink business. One change required major investment in new equipment, at least new to us. It was the appearance of the 32 oz. glass bottle. It was a bit difficult to put a 32 ounce bottle into a machine that would only take a 6 ½ oz. Coke bottle.

Other changes included getting into the fountain business while continuing to provide drinks to football stadiums and basketball gyms. And there was a new version of our old customer, the service station. Now they not only sold three grades of gasoline, but sandwiches, candy, food ready to go, and lots of other stuff. This was a prime outlet for us to provide new counter top units that could dispense from 4 to 8 different drinks.

Looking back, I must say I'm so pleased to have been part of a family business which started in 1904 and remained active for 84 years. Kids and grownups alike loved to peer through the huge windows at the bottling plant and watch the process. It always made us happy to see their smiling faces through the windows. Because Jacksonville has meant so much to me and to my family; I wanted to make a difference which is why I served as Mayor twice and was also County Judge. Jacksonville is a wonderful place to live.

Recollections of Jacksonville

Memoirs by Harry Tilley

The Far Reaching Impact of a Fred Douglas High School Education

I was born November 24, 1950, in Jacksonville, Texas. I was raised in Gallatin, Texas, about eight miles east of Jacksonville in a small community with one family-owned general store. My father and mother, Odie and Gladys Williams, were very concerned about all eleven of us children getting a higher education.

Dad was employed by the Southern Pacific Railroad Company (with an 8th grade education). He worked for over 33 years before retiring, and my mother was a retired teacher and full-time housewife. We lived on 160 acres of farmland (now forest) where we grew produce such as tomatoes, onions, greens, sweet potatoes, etc. to sell downtown in Jacksonville, Texas.

Simple things like pushing car tires around the yard, pretending we were driving, playing hopscotch, making wooden pistols, bow and arrows to play cowboys and Indians, gave us so much joy. One of our favorite things to do growing up was to look through catalogs and creating a wish list of things we were going to buy when we became successful. My wish list consisted of things like houses, cars, and clothes.

Education was something my mother was big on. She always made sure we got our schoolwork done. I attended Fred Douglass H.S. from 1966-1969. At Fred Douglass H.S. there were male teachers whom I wanted to emulate such as Mr. P.H. Crawford (chemistry teacher, coach, Boy Scout leader organization called the Explorers), Mr. B. T. Finely (coach, math teacher, science teacher and electrician). Mr. Crawford and Mr. Finley ran the swimming pool at Lincoln Park where I became a lifeguard. Mr. Hayes (coach, world history teacher, and barber) Mr. Mules (agriculture teacher) and Mr. Melvin Davis (band director) made it possible for me to get a band work scholarship to attend Prairie View A&M University. There was also Mr. Wayne Craddock (algebra & trigonometry teacher) who prepared me and five other boys with skills and tried to persuade us to go to West Point Military Academy in New York, where men were trained to become generals, though we had other plans. And finally, Professor Clyde Christopher (math teacher) who was so heavy into math that he went on to teach mathematic at Prairie View A&M University. All of them were very active and important men in the community. I often would quote some of their phrases they would say. They were eager to share their experiences with me that influenced me in seeking to aim higher in life.

I can recall Nipsey Russell (comedian/actor) saying, "If they can make penicillin out of mold and cheese, they ought to make something out of you." I can credit my success and my sibling's success to these great teachers at Fred Douglass H.S.

Recollections of Jacksonville

Memoirs by Billy Jack Williams, Jr.

Reminiscence Room Biographies

As a part of the Jacksonville Sesquicentennial celebration on Saturday, October 22, 2022, a group of local people with long memories was asked to share their experiences of living in our community. They formed a panel that met in the Neighbors' Coffee shop to share stories with each other and listeners in the audience surrounding them. Dr. Deborah Burkett led the panel discussion and then invited the audience to ask questions. Several presenters were in their 90's or nearly 90 years old. The yarns they told were worth recording and leaving for posterity. The *"Do You Remember When"* program was enthusiastically received by the crowd that came to reminisce with the panel about the lives they had lived.

Each person was especially chosen to be part of this program because of their active part in local activities and notable events. Jacksonville Progress reporter Mrs. Mary Beth Scallon interviewed each panelist and wrote an extended biographical article about them that was published in the local paper, along with their identifying photos. Scallion's stories have been collected and preserved for your enjoyment and education.

Photos of the event that took place on the Sesquicentennial Homecoming Day on 10/22/22 have been added of the celebrated discussions of old times.

Some of Jacksonville's Living Legacies Gather at Neighbor's Coffee
During the Homecoming Celebration to Tell Their Stories

Mary Alice Bone Adamson
A Legacy of Healthy Bones

The study and practice of medicine has played a part in the life of Mary Alice Bone Adamson as far back as she can remember – and probably before that. Her father, Dr. J. N. Bone, practiced medicine in Douglass and Atoy. Her grandfather, Dr. R. D. Bone, had an office in Tennessee before moving to Texas. After moving to Texas, Dr. R. D. Bone volunteered to serve in the Civil War as a surgeon for soldiers. During that time, his letters home to his wife were full of details and also requests. One such letter implored his wife to send bedding, because the soldiers had no pillows. Another asked her to send a mule, because service for the men involved walking long miles. The letters are now preserved in the historical archives of the Stephen F. Austin University Library.

Adamson said she believes her grandfather came to Texas with a group of Cumberland Presbyterian Church followers, a branch of the denomination that was prevalent at the time in Tennessee. The group settled near Larissa, a town that eventually became Mt. Selman. Many of the early members of that group are buried in a cemetery there that is still called Larissa Cemetery. "There's a lot of Bones out there," Dr. Adamson joked. Her father went back to Tennessee for medical school. When he returned to Cherokee County after the death of his father, there were two other doctors practicing in the county. Her father's practice also involved the dispensing of medicine.

She relayed a story about an incident in her father's practice. "One of his patients was a boy whose mother sent him to my dad. My dad put the powdered medicine in a page of his prescription pad. It was some kind of medicine that you just added water to when you took it. The boy asked how much he owed, and my father told him he didn't owe him anything. "The boy told him he would get in trouble from his mother if he didn't pay something, so he pulled out a dime. My father took it and said later it was the cheapest payment he had ever received on a medical bill," she said.

When Dr. J.N. Bone, her dad, moved to Jacksonville from Larissa, he was one of four doctors who opened the Cherokee Sanitorium – not sanitarium, she was quick to add. The name later was changed to Nan Travis Hospital to honor the mother of Dr. Travis, one of the four doctors. Adamson's grandmother died when her mother was a teenager, and her mother married soon after. When her husband and baby died during the flu epidemic of 1918, Adamson's mother went to college in South Carolina to become a nurse. There she met a Miss Baumburger, who later married and became Mrs. McMinn. Mrs. McMinn eventually became the Superintendent of Nurses for Nan Travis Hospital, and she invited Adamson's mother to join her in Jacksonville. She did, and during her tenure at the hospital, she met and married Adamson's father, who was by then a widower with two daughters who became Adamson's older sisters after she was born a few years later.

After graduating from Jacksonville High School, Adamson – Mary Alice Bone at the time – attended Trinity University, and then went to Southwest Medical School in Dallas. While there, she married John Adamson, "I went to school for my M.D., and got my MRS," she said, adding that she did finish her residency at Parkland Memorial Hospital in Dallas before moving back to East Texas to practice medicine. John Adamson, known by most as Bob, practiced law and eventually was appointed by the State of Texas to serve as the 22nd Judicial District Judge for Texas, a position he held for many years. The couple was married just short of 55 years.

Her professional name was Dr. Bone, and she practiced medicine first for Sunset Care Center as house physician. After three years there, she joined a team of doctors to work in the new Travis Clinic on the loop, where she stayed for 11 years until the facility closed. Following that, she had a private practice in the same building with Dr. Story and Dr. Austin Weaver, who were later joined by Dr. Craig Weaver. After retiring from private practice 11 years later, she became the Cherokee County Health Department Director, where she served for 20 years before her next retirement. But she was not quite done with the practice of medicine. Even before retirement, she had begun volunteer service at the Mission Home Clinic in Bullard, joining her brother who was a doctor. After serving there a few years, she finally decided to rest and retire once more. "I hung up my stethoscope at 90," she said, her words reflecting a legacy of service and dedication to the health of East Texas.

Shelley Cleaver

Cleaver Finds Community Service a Recipe for Success

He may have been called by other things, but Shelley Cleaver has probably never been called late to supper. In collaboration with Cherokee County artist and historian, Lurlene Bowden, Cleaver has co-authored four cookbooks, mostly focusing on recipes from his family, with tidbits about Lone Star, the area in which he was born. "I was born in the house that is still there," he said. "My grandpa lived upstairs. His birthday was Dec. 25, so my Mama was trying to hold on till then, but I couldn't wait. "My daddy went on the horse and buggy to get Dr. Barnett, and I was born Dec. 24. I was only 12 pounds. They had been baling cotton that day, so they weighed me on the cotton scales." Cleaver explained that Lonestar was located in the area near the intersection of CR 235 and CR 2274, near Ponta. The community began to disappear after the railroad came to Ponta, and Highway 79 was built.

When he was a few years older, his daddy took a job at Byrd Brothers Dodge & Plymouth in Jacksonville, so the family moved to South Street in Jacksonville, just outside the city limits. He attended East Side Elementary until the seventh grade, and then went to Jacksonville High School until he graduated in 1952. "In 1952, I was on the state relay team," he said. "We set a record in Austin. You can see that picture at the Tomato Bowl." Following graduation, Cleaver joined the Army, but not before marrying his high school sweetheart, Laura Jane Holcomb. Her dad owned Holcomb Motors in Jacksonville. After joining the Army, he was sent to Korea for two years, where he served as a crane operator in the Aviation Engineers. When his active service ended, he served six years in reserve duty, but was never called back to active service.

He and Jane Cleaver had a daughter and two sons before she passed. In 1968, he married Jannell Dickson, and they were married until she died in 2003. Jannell, a widower, had four sons, and Cleaver raised them with his other children. He and Jannell also eventually had another son, Michael. "Four of my boys are still living," Cleaver said on his honeymoon, the couple rode in Cleaver's 1958 Edsel. "I could shift with my left arm, and put my right arm around my bride," he said, his eyes twinkling as he recalled the fond memory. For some reason that is unknown to him, some woman has created a YouTube video that calls Cleaver "the rough road that gave the Edsel a bad name." Referencing the video, Cleaver said he doesn't know where she got the idea, but that anyone who wants to see the video can find it on YouTube.

One of his favorite stories in the Volume 4 cookbook, labeled "Pistol Packing Mama," details the story of Cherokee County Sheriff Bill Brunt, who was killed by a bootlegger in 1939. Brunt's wife, Mary Dear, assumed his duties, deciding not to run again in 1940 when the term expired. A song, "Pistol Packing Mama," became a billboard hit in the mid-1940s, and some believe it referred to Brunt's wife – but others refute that story, according to Cleaver. The cookbooks, published and illustrated by Bowden and co-written by Cleaver, can be purchased directly from Shelley Cleaver by calling 903-586-4311.

Cleaver, who also goes by the name "Shamrock," is active in the Cherokee County Historical Commission, and is proud to have served on a number of efforts to improve the quality of life in Cherokee County and particularly, in Jacksonville. He had a part in getting the bond passed to rebuild the Tomato Bowl, and has participated in a number of historical markers being placed around the city. One of those denotes the history of the old post office, now being used as the location for Postmasters Coffee. "The old post office didn't have any room to park," he said. "That's why there was a new one built." Cleaver explained that Herman Glass was still the postmaster when the new one was built. Glass was appointed by President Lyndon Baines Johnson, and when he retired, he was recognized to be the

Recollections of Jacksonville

oldest postmaster who had been appointed by a president. "They used to all be appointed that way," Cleaver said.

As a member of the Cherokee County Historical Commission, Cleaver was involved in securing a historical marker for the post office, which was built in 1933. The building now is officially recognized in the National Registry of Historical Buildings. He was also involved in ensuring a marker that had been taken from the Caddo Indian Mounds Park was restored to its rightful location. The marker had been stolen, and was later found in a garage in another county. It was turned over to the Texas Rangers, who returned it to Cherokee County. As a veteran, Cleaver is also involved in the Lone Star Military Resource Group, and can be seen at most community gatherings showing his support. The 87-year-old says it is his great desire to be of service.

Dr. Charles Creed
His 93 Year Retrospective

Although he is not a native of Jacksonville, Dr. Charles Creed and his wife, Jeanette, came to the city as quickly as they could, finding its residents to be warm and welcoming. Creed, a local dentist who is now retired, grew up in Warren, Arkansas, but came to Texas after high school to attend Baylor University. After completing his studies at BU, he went to dental school in Dallas. Because he had a deferred draft status, he knew he would soon be called up to duty; so instead, he volunteered and joined the United States Air Force, offering his services. He was sworn in on the day he graduated from dental school.

In the meantime, he had met Jeanette. She laughs that the union was meant to be. "I went to the school to get cheap dental care," she said. "I came back with a husband." The couple married in 1954, just after the Korean War had ended. When Dr. Creed's military orders came, he was assigned to serve in Japan. "I took a bride abroad," he quipped. When they returned stateside, they began to look for a town in which to settle. They wanted a small town, with a friendly atmosphere. They looked first in Arkansas, to be near his parents, but no place seemed suitable, so they drove into Texas and began a search that took a few weeks. They liked what they saw in Jacksonville, and the people they met, and chose to begin their residence in the town. "The people were so friendly," Jeanette said. "In fact, we weren't here two hours when Frank Burroughs and B.B. Fields showed up to welcome us." She added that Burroughs was the minister of Central Baptist Church, where she and Dr. Creed joined almost immediately, and where they have remained active ever since.

Dr. Creed's first dental office was in the old First National Bank building that was located on Main Street. That building was eventually torn down; the bank was located across the street, and then purchased by Austin Bank. While Dr. Creed's office was in the old building, however, he occupied an area on an upper floor, where he could look out and see many of the industries that have now disappeared from the city's landscape, such as J.C. Penney, Marja's Brassiere, and the Liberty Hotel. He moved to the new Austin Bank building when that facility was completed, and operated his dentistry practice there for about 10 years, before opening his own office on Highway 79, sharing the purchase and building with Dr. James Adams.

He said he is grateful to the Austin Family for having always been supportive. "The Austins have always been very helpful," he said. "They made a place for me; even loaned us the money to build the new clinic." Jacksonville at the time was a busy place. Dr. Creed remembers some of the more notable perks of living in the city. "Jacksonville was more of a medical center," he said. "We had Nan Travis Hospital and Travis Clinic, also Newburn Hospital. People would drive for miles to visit the clinic. Of course, that was before Tyler's medical facilities grew." His wife added that most people did not drive to Tyler to shop back then, because there was ample shopping in Jacksonville. "The downtown was bustling. You could buy clothes; a man could buy a suit, a woman could buy a dress. There was even a hat shop and three jewelry stores. We had Lang's, The Diamond Shop and Lowell's Jewelry. And, the Liberty Hotel had good food, before it burned," Jeanette said, adding that the town also had Nichols Photography Studio and photography by Mack Bagley. With all that busyness, the town needed the overpass that was eventually built. "People needed to get to the hospital, and to their jobs," Dr. Creed said, "and they were being stopped by the train that ran through town."
  When he opened his office on Highway 79, he was the first dentist in town to utilize a dental hygienist, using the services of a Distributive Education (D.E.) student, Pam Waites. "I think this was probably the beginning of the time when people started going to the dentist for more than just extractions and dentures," he said. Because he knows so much of the history of

Jacksonville, Dr. Creed serves weekly as a volunteer at the Love's Lookout Welcome Center. He also has served, and continues to serve, as a director of Austin Bank. His past service includes serving on the Jacksonville ISD school board for 16 years; as a director for Nan Travis Hospital board for many years – too many to recall, he said; and president of the East Texas Dental Society. Dr. Creed also served two, three-year terms on the Executive Board of the Baptist General Convention of Texas, and Jeanette Creed separately served the same amount of time on that board. His service also included a year stint as a trustee with the Texas Association of School Boards, and he has been a member of Jacksonville's Rotary Club since 1957. "I'm the oldest member in Rotary now," he laughed.

The Creeds' son, Dr. Brad Creed, is president of Campbell University in North Carolina, and their daughter, Sarah, has been a teacher for 30 years. The couple also has four grandchildren, and two great-grandchildren. "We've been blessed. Jacksonville has been a good place to live and raise children," Dr. Creed said, with his wife in agreement. "People don't have to go to Dallas or Houston for their quality of life. Lots of people want to come here. "We're here for the duration."

Barbara Crossman
Former Librarian Shares a Few Pages of History

Jacksonville Public Library has changed locations twice in the years since Barbara Crossman came to Jacksonville. The 90-year-old, who doesn't mind telling her age, moved to the city after meeting her late husband, Robert Nathan Crossman, Jr. (Bob), on a blind date.
"I was attending the University Of Houston School Of Architecture," she said. "I grew up in Eldorado, Arkansas, a town not too far from where Dr. Charles Creed grew up. After college in Denver, I went to Southern Methodist University near Dallas, and then went to UH. I wanted to be an architect."

The couple married in 1957, and after three years moved to Jacksonville. Bob had served in Vietnam with the United States Air Force, and had graduated from Rice University. Their first child, Robert Nathan Crossman III, was already born. Their daughter, Barbara Ann, and son, Charles Nathan, were born within the next few years. At the time, the library was located in the City Park, where the Vanishing Texana Museum continues service to the public. Although Crossman had been a stay-at-home mom for many years, she decided to go to work after her children were almost high school age, and her first and last job in Jacksonville was at the library, where she stayed until her retirement 30 years later.

She began work under the direction of then-librarian, Betty Sheffield. "I showed films to nursing homes and businesses. I carried a 16 millimeter projector, a speaker and a stand in my station wagon. I showed films you could borrow from the library for free. I also helped with projects. For instance, we helped put together a Union Catalog, so we could share with librarians in nearby towns and exchange ideas or places to order new books. Then, computers came along, and that put a stop to that, she said.

During Betty Sheffield's tenure, she decided the library needed a new location, so Crossman and others on the staff helped with the drive to get that accomplished. Although the sale of bonds was proposed, the idea was not approved by voters, and plans were put back on the drawing board. Jacksonville resident John Allen Templeton was instrumental in the drive to get donations, and the Meadows Foundation also gave money. Crossman said a new library was built on South Jackson Street, where the former Buddie's Supermarket had been located. "They hired George Rogers, a great architectural firm from Marshall, and it was built in 1983," she said.

Her first position with the library was part-time work, but in 1984, she became a full-time employee, doing whatever needed to be done. When Betty Sheffield retired, Betty Landon took over the reins as director. "She was the first librarian in Jacksonville to actually have a library science degree," Crossman said. That was what Betty Sheffield had hoped for." Landon stayed three years, and then a Mrs. Simon was hired. "When she left, about 1992, I finally decided to apply for the job," Crossman said, "Then I stayed until 2015."

The now-retired librarian said she had been aware of the need for the Jackson Street library to be relocated, because of its lucrative real estate value. She had been researching locations when it was decided that the city would relocate it downtown. "I didn't realize the Norman Center would come available," she said, noting that a library's facilities would of necessity be able to withstand the weight of a large number of books. "They are very heavy," she said.

She said a librarian's role is important, explaining that it is necessary to consider the needs of patrons. "A librarian has to think about what their patrons really want in the way of a library and how they can furnish that information in a way easily attained, and do so with a variety of mixed media," she said. Because of her interest and studies in architecture, Crossman has always enjoyed living in Jacksonville. "I like old houses and railroads," she said. "Because of the railroads, the towns grew. Once the railroads started going away, some of the towns changed. In Jacksonville, some of the commerce from farm production and sales started to go away.

Then businesses such as Marja's Brassiere Factory, Mr. Fine and Nichols-Kusan developed."

She said she is proud that the library has been able to provide computers for clients to use, and also to offer classes teaching those clients how to use the technology. She said she is also grateful to the Jacksonville Library Association and the Friends of the Library for their assistance through the years, and the Gates Foundation for donating the computers. These days, she enjoys spending time with her children and four grandchildren. She also loves working in her garden, playing with cats who visit her yard, and watching birds. "I'm just a nature lover," she said. "I always enjoyed helping people in the library. I liked doing research, and I have always felt a part of the community.

Barbara Hugghins
Volunteer Who Continues Community Work

Barbara Hugghins doesn't know what it means to stop working. Although she has been officially retired after 40 years of ministry at the First United Methodist Church in Jacksonville, she continues to fill her days with acts of service. She can be found every Tuesday morning at the park station at Love's Lookout, where she serves as a hostess, greeting visitors and making sure they have a cup of coffee, if they want, and that they learn a little bit about the area's history.

In 1985, she was certified as a Diaconal Minister, and she still fulfills some of those duties. "I still do weddings and funerals," she said. "During COVID, I conducted quite a few graveside services." She came to Jacksonville in 1948 to attend Lon Morris College, where she met and married Gordon L. Hugghins. The couple traveled many places with the U.S. Navy, returning in four years to Jacksonville, where his family owned and operated Nichols Studio and Hugghins Photography, and where she assisted Gordon in his work.

Their children include Gayla Jeanne Hugghins, Glynda Jane Thompson, Gordon Jeffrey Hugghins, Angela Jo Driggs and Gordon Leonard Hugghins. Eleven grandchildren have been born into the family, and a great-grandchild is on the way. Barbara Hugghins received her Associate of Arts degree from LMC in 1950; Bachelor of Arts for University of Texas-Tyler in 1981, and her Masters of Arts at UTT in 1985. In addition to her ministerial certification, she was ordained a Deacon in the UMC in 1998.

Her service in the church, as well as in the community, includes leading volunteers in outreach, mission trips and projects, including team projects at United Methodist Committee Overseas Relief in Baldwin, LA; McCurdy

School in Espanola, NM; Mercy Ships Headquarters in Van, and others. "At Mercy Ships, we did yard work, helped in the kitchen, sorted eyeglasses – whatever was needed. It is a learning experience for volunteers, and helps (the program) as well. Of course, our group usually also gave a monetary donation," she said, adding that anyone with an interest should stop by the facility for a tour.

Barbara and Gordon Hugghins were also foster parents to several children. "We had one girl who stayed with us for eight years, and I am still in contact with her," Barbara said, noting that at the time, foster parents were not allowed to adopt their foster children, although that rule now has been lifted somewhat. She was one of the founders of the Soup Kitchen at PROJECT HOPE, which began with a Crockpot of Soup and Sandwiches. She has been active in the Jacksonville Ministerial Alliance, Cherokee County Child and Protective Family Services Board Rainbow Room, and Court Appointed Special Advocates for children.

When her husband died many years ago, Barbara still had one teenager at home, but becoming a single parent did not slow her down. In fact, her involvement in numerous acts of service earned her many honors, including being named as Lon Morris College Distinguished Alumni (95-96); Texas Conference of the UMC Christian Education award (1995); and 1998 Citizen of the Year by Jacksonville Chamber of Commerce.

The Love's Lookout "gig" is just one of the many activities in which Hugghins participates. She is on the board for the Vanishing Texana Museum, is involved with the county's Genealogy Group, is a member of a book club and enjoys meeting with friends in several birthday clubs. She directs a Grief Recovery Class at FUMC. She serves each week in the Food Pantry at the church, as well as the clothes closet at the Department of Child and Protective Services, and is still a member of the Cherokee County Child and Protective Services. When Lon Morris closed a few years ago, she and historian Deborah Burkett traveled to Conroe to retrieve some historical items that had belonged to LMC, but that had been stored in Conroe at the LMC Historical Archives. "We picked up books, pictures, etc. It took several trips, but we celebrated with a big party when we were done. The items are available now for anyone to view, at the Cherokee Historical Museum in Rusk. Some of them are also available at the Bridwell Library at SMU Perkins School of Theology; SFA University Library; Vanishing Texana Museum and also the Jacksonville Public Library," she said.

She said she enjoys traveling with her children, and her hobbies include knitting baby blankets to give away, and reading. Hugghins remembers celebrating Jacksonville's Centennial in 1972, and looks forward to doing the same for the Sesquicentennial. "Jacksonville has been a wonderful community to live in, to raise a family, and to serve," she said.

Hallie Peoples
Longtime Resident Shares Childhood Memories

Hallie Jewell Henry Peoples remembers walking all the way from Highway 175 on Sundays to eat at the Dairy Queen near the Tomato Bowl on Sunday afternoons – but only after church, of course. She also remembers that the Palace and the Rialto were the names of the two theaters in town. Near the Rialto was a hamburger shop. She couldn't remember the name, but still remembers how good those burgers tasted. "Those were the best burgers," she said. "We looked forward to going to the movies, so we could go get a hamburger there afterward."

Peoples is now retired, but served more than 50 years as a Registered Respiratory Therapist for the former Nan Travis Hospital, which now serves as the University of Texas Medical Center after going through several name changes and a new building. Before she earned her respiratory therapist registration, however, she was an LVN. She served as a school nurse at Jacksonville ISD, and also at Rusk, then went to work for a year at Rusk State Hospital. After taking maternity leave from there, a friend talked her into helping out in the program at Nan Travis.

"My friend, Sybil Lovelady, had been my 'big sister' in nursing school and she set up the respiratory therapy program at Nan Travis," she said. "She talked me into helping out one summer, and I fell in love with what I was doing." She loved the work so much that she decided to get the formal education she needed for the registry, and so attended Jarvis Christian College, and then Tyler Junior College. She received her associate's degree in two years, and then applied for and earned the registered title.

Although she attended North Bolton Street Christian Church as a child, she joined Churchill CME Church after marrying Hiram – who goes simply by "H" – Peoples. The two have been active in church work and in community events. She remembers a lot of things about Jacksonville. One particular memory is eating whiting, which is a type of fish, at a restaurant near the A&P, located where the First National Bank was later built, and then was replaced by Austin Bank. "My friend and I said we would never eat whiting again, we ate it so much when we were younger. But then Mr. Melvin opened a place on Lincoln Street, and we ate it some more. I think Mr. Melvin's last name was Silmon," she said.

She remembers going to the theater and sitting upstairs in the "colored" section, but said she never felt discriminated against in Jacksonville. "Even when we integrated, we didn't have any problems. We all supported each other," Peoples said. "I remember the band at Fred Douglass High School had blue and gold uniforms, even though our colors were purple and white. We got hand-me-downs from Jacksonville ISD. But then Mr. Melvin Davis, one of the band directors, arranged for our band to get purple and white uniforms, and we were so proud. "Of course, I was a cheerleader, I wasn't in the band, but I remember when the band got those uniforms." Peoples added that a picture of her cheering squad can now be seen in the collection of pictures at the Tomato Bowl. She recalls there was a youth center on Main Street called the Wig-Wam, for students at Jacksonville High School. Kids in the Lincoln Park area, where she lived, attended Fred Douglass High School, and their team was the Dragons. "Mr. Richard Stone, the lawyer, got us our own youth center on Elberta Street. We called it the Dragons' Den," she said.

Her husband, H, worked for Jacksonville High School for several years. He also served as a District Scout Executive for awhile, and taught Adult Basic Education at Rusk State Hospital.

Although she had her own work to do, she occasionally helped out her husband during a time when he owned a limousine service. She remembers a funny incident that happened back then.

"I took a load of people to town. When I got ready to take them back, I couldn't back out with the limousine, so I had to have one of them help me," she said, laughing at the memory.

As an adult, Hallie Peoples was the first black woman to have been named a director of any kind at Nan Travis Hospital, serving as the Director of Physical Therapy for many years. She finds it ironic that the former Nan Travis building once faced Ragsdale Street, but when the building was remodeled, it faced south. After being remodeled a second time years later, it now faces back to Ragsdale Street. She has served on a number of community boards, including the Chamber of Commerce and the Child Welfare Board. She also was in charge of the tomato-eating contest at the Tomato Fest for several years.

She recently wrote and presented a short history of Fred Douglass High School for that school system's anniversary celebration. These days, she and H stay active in their church. They have served at the local, district, regional and national levels in varying roles, and both love working with young people. She is proud that her nephew, Charlvin Doty is now pastor at Kingdom Christian Center, in the building that once housed the Presbyterian Church. She fondly recalls going to church with her parents, Julian and Ida Belle Henry. "When we were growing up, church was the center of everything," she said. "We had no choice. Parents told us what to do. Nowadays, kids tell their parents what to do. I'm glad I had that kind of background. God is first and foremost in my life. I am in awe of His goodness, grace and mercy," she said. She and her husband are celebrating 59 years of marriage this month, and she credits some advice from her dad for that success. "My daddy said the family that prays together, stays together," she said. "And I guess it worked."

Recollections of Jacksoville

Sarah Robinson
Daycare Owner Fondly Recalls School Days

Sarah Robinson has been involved with the nurture and care of children for most of her life. She and her late husband, John, owned and operated Kids "R" Us, a daycare located on Ragsdale Street, for 33 years. Although John worked as a conductor for Union Pacific railroad for 32 years, Sarah said it was her husband's idea to open the daycare. "I had been working for several years for Golda Pugh, who owned Pugh's Play & Learn. I wanted to start my own daycare, but I told my husband probably nobody would come, because Golda was so popular," she said. "My husband said, 'Well, we have been involved with kids all our married life. You just go ahead and open that daycare. There are enough kids in Jacksonville for you and Ms. Pugh both.' So I did," she said.

She was quick to add that she wanted it run a certain way. "It was a Christian daycare," she said. "We started the day with prayer. I wanted my kids to learn the Bible." Robinson was both administrator and kindergarten teacher at the school. She is proud that many of the students she taught have gone on to achieve notable success. Among them are bank officers, nurses, nurse practitioners and teachers. One student she particularly remembers is Darrel Thompson. He is now a bank officer in Texas, although she could not immediately remember the town. "When he was a junior at Jacksonville High School, he nominated me to the 2002 Who's Who among American Teachers," she said. "I have the book with my biography and picture. "He was a special kid and made me so proud. That's the highlight of being in the daycare business."

She remembered other names, as well: Shynonda Newsome, who is now a nurse practitioner in Tyler; a niece, Samantha Scott, who is a nurse practitioner in California, and Tyson Cannon.
"Tyson is a captain in the Army," she said. "He got his four-year degree, and then joined the Army." Robinson was reluctant to just give the four names, indicating she was proud of all her "kids." When she was younger, both she and John Ragsdale coached in various youth leagues in the city of Jacksonville. Sarah coached girls' softball, soccer and basketball; John coached softball and basketball. She also played softball in an adult league sponsored by Galaxy Boatworks, and together, the couple was active in teaching kids at Seminary Heights Church of Christ.

In 2006, Robinson ran for a place on the Jacksonville ISD school board. Although her bid was unsuccessful, she nevertheless expressed her opinion regarding discipline in the schools. "I strongly believe that discipline begins at home, and it should continue on into our schools. It has gotten to the point that there is no discipline in so many of our homes, and this non-discipline is carried into our schools. The children have no respect for themselves or the teachers. If there is no discipline, there is no respect. If there is no respect, there won't be any learning," she said.
After her husband died in 2019, she tried to keep working and operating the daycare, but her heart was just not in it. "There were too many memories after 51 years of being married," she said. When COVID hit, she closed Kids "R" Us, and decided finally to just sell it. The school now operates as Creative Little Angels, with a new owner. She has moved to Midlothian to live with her son, but gets back to Jacksonville as often as she can.

The longtime educator said she believes her own success was due to her belief in God, and it was a belief she tried to instill in her kindergarten students and the other children who attended her daycare. "If you don't have God as a part of your life, your chances of success are slim to none," she said. "Today's mentality calls evil, good and good, evil. A quote from Bessie Anderson Stanley, an American writer who died in 1952, seems to address the sum of the years Sarah Robinson has spent educating and working with children: "What constitutes success? She has achieved success who has lived well; laughed often and loved much; who has gained the respect of intelligent people and the love of little children; who has filled her niche and accomplished her task; who has left the world better than she found it; who has always looked for the best in others and given the best she had." (from For Women by Women, Dayspring 2011).

Recollections of Jacksonville

Harry Gordon Tilley
Former Coca-Cola exec the real thing

It would be easy to make a wisecrack and say Harry Gordon Tilley keeps his information bottled up inside, but the truth is, he doesn't mind sharing how the history of his family began in a bottling plant – or at least, the part of his history that began more than 118 years ago. His father, Harry Park Tilley, known to his friends as "Pat," bought the bottling operation in 1904 that was located in back of Ambrose Johnson's Drugstore in downtown Jacksonville. Pat Tilley's father, George Tilley, had moved to Jacksonville when the town was relocated to the current location from the former site in the area known as Larissa. George Tilley and his business partner had a mercantile business in Larissa, titled "Tilley & Suttles," but were instrumental in moving the first building into the new location of the City of Jacksonville, or that's the rumor, anyway. His great-grandson, Harry Gordon Tilley, said he was given the information from a prominent house painter in Jacksonville. "That first building was a saloon," he said.

When Pat Tilley bought the bottling operation from the drugstore, he operated it initially at that location. Eventually, he moved to a new spot on South Bolton, where the Coca-Cola plant was established that operated for many years. Pat Tilley died in 1948, and his son, F. Gordon Tilley, assumed ownership of the company. This was during World War II, and Gordon Tilley created a new way of making "crowns," or bottle caps, since metal was scarce. "He would get cans from the dietitians at the schools, cut the sides off, and use a stamping machine (he invented) that was operated by a foot pedal," Harry Tilley said. "You could get 5 or 6 crowns from one can." Harry Tilley went to work for his dad in 1944, when he was 12 years old. His principal job was putting corks in the bottle. His friend, John Clark, also helped. "We would put a drop of glue on the cork, it would go in the machine, we would press and it would seal," he said, bragging about earning 12 ½ cents per hour.

Harry Tilley joined the US Army in 1955, after completing his college education. He joined as a second lieutenant, and became a first lieutenant before his active military term ended in 1957. He also served in the Army reserves for two years after the discharge. In 1969, when Gordon Tilley died, Harry Tilley became president and CEO, and operated the business until 1988, when the business was sold. In the 1970s, Harry Tilley ran for and won a seat on the Jacksonville City Council. At that time, city council members elected the mayor from among the group serving on the council. Other members at that time were Philip Pavletich, J.E. Brown, Tally Nichols, and later, F.E. Shinalt. Council members rotated serving as mayor. When a city-wide election divided the city into four precincts, the mayor was elected by the city-at-large, and Pavletich served as the first elected mayor, followed by Tilley, who served two two-year terms.

During that time, Tilley met and married his wife, Norma. "We met at some ribbon-cuttings while I was mayor," he said. "She was wearing a red jacket, like the other ladies who wore them at the ribbon-cuttings." His wife of 34 years reminded him that they had actually briefly met before that time, when they happened to be at the courthouse at the same time, but got to know each other better at the ribbon-cuttings. "He likes to tell about the red jackets," she laughed.
After the business sold, Tilley was elected Cherokee County judge, a position he held for eight years. He was presiding over the county commissioners meeting Sept. 11, 2011. "There was so much going on that day," he said, recalling that there were a lot of prayers being said that day and many days after.

These days, Tilley keeps busy with volunteer work. For several years, he served on the board of Jacksonville Literacy Council. Currently, he stops in at the Helping Others Pursue Enrichment (HOPE) center almost every day, helping in whatever way is necessary. Since the late 1990s, he has served as the Chairman of Jacksonville Housing Authority, an entity that helps to provide rent subsidies for low and moderate-income families. He is skilled in technology repair and the use of computers to make life easier, and has been instrumental in getting some computers donated to teach classes at either HOPE or the Housing Authority offices which are located at the center. COVID restrictions during the past couple of years have hampered that project, but he is hopeful that the organizations can soon offer classes that will enable students to learn some computer skills to benefit job search and training.

He echoed those who have previously been interviewed for the Sesquicentennial Celebration Reminiscence Room panel, saying Jacksonville is a great place to live. "I do appreciate the people of Jacksonville for electing me to the position of mayor," he said, "and for the people of Cherokee County for having the confidence to allow me to serve as county judge for eight years."

Recollections of Jacksoville

SECTION 2

Sesquicentennial Celebration 2022

This following pages document the different celebrations that the citizens of Jacksonville came together to pay tribute to our beloved town. Pictured are faces of the past, present and future of Jacksonville.

Promoting a Hometown Celebration
Jan -April 2022

Promoting Our Celebration

The Jacksonville Sesquicentennial celebration actually began on January 1, 2022. The Cherokee County Historical Commission, in cooperation with the Jacksonville Vanishing Texanna Museum, published a 2022 calendar that was dedicated to Jacksonville with our city's historical photos and dates listed every month of the year. Preparation for this calendar was begun in early 2021. The calendar was finished in November 2021 and offered for sale to the public, in time for immediate use when 2022 began. The city of Jacksonville is grateful for the support of the Cherokee County Historical Commission, especially Dr. Deborah Burkett, and the city museum curator, Larry Lydick. The calendar is now a historical record of our city. Because of the calendar's importance, a copy of it will be placed in the bicentennial time capsule. The calendar cover page is pictured below.

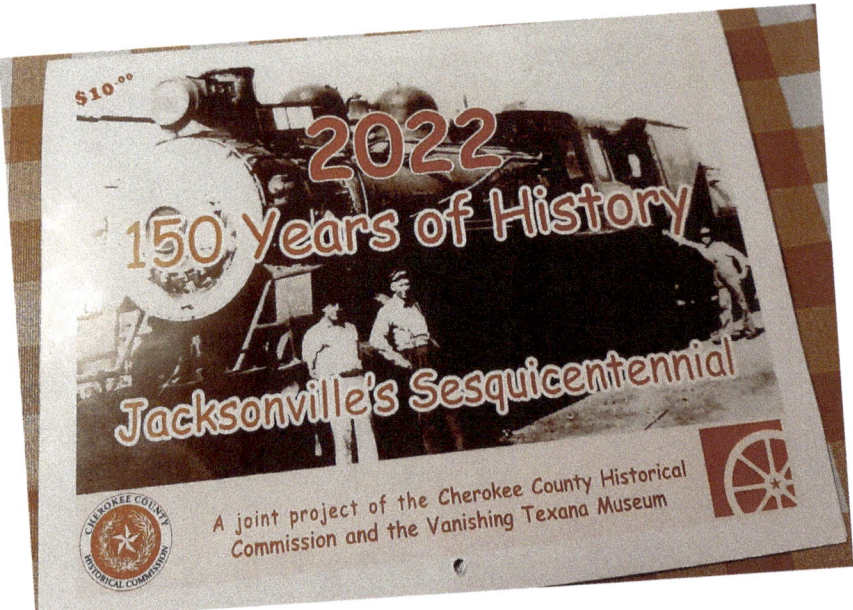

Hometown Newspaper

The other sesquicentennial observances that began in January 2022 were the publications in the Jacksonville Progress, and in the Cherokeean in Rusk, the weekly publications of the Recollections of Jacksonville stories. The memoirs were printed from the first week of January to the first week of November. There were eight additional stories about the senior panelists who were featured in the Reminiscence Room program. These eight biographies and 44 memoirs provided a total of 50 printed sesquicentennial stories. The goal of the Recollections project was to leave behind a journalistic record of the period since the city's centennial in 1972. Gathering these stories was a yearlong job. Recollections of Jacksonville writers had to be recruited, assisted with story writing, and then scheduled for publication in the two newspapers. The results were personal testimonies and tributes which were gratifying to read as a permanent record of our era in Jacksonville. A sample of a printed newspaper recollection story is shown below:

Recollections of Jacksoville

Heritage Center of Cherokee County Sesquicentennial Display

Betty Marcontell, the museum director of the Heritage Center located in Rusk, created a historical display to honor the Jacksonville Sesquicentennial. The artistic display showed artifacts and photos of our city's past. Mrs. Marcontell invited the Jacksonville Sesquicentennial committee to come for a private showing of the display. The committee members enthusiastically praised the content of the museum's splendid arrangement when they visited the site in April 2022.

Committee members from left to right are:
Dr. Deborah Burkett, Mrs. Tracy Wallace, Mr. Johnny Helm, City Manager James Hubbard, Dr. Sam Hopkins, Mrs. Kathleen Stanfill, Mrs. Charlie Esco, Mrs. Cassie Devillier.

Centennial Time Capsule Opening
May 11th, 2022

Recollections of Jacksoville

Opening the Centennial Time Capsule

The centennial 1972 capsule was buried on May 11, 1972, in the southeast corner of the Hazel Tilton city park. Exactly 50 years later as part of the city's sesquicentennial celebration, the time capsule was dug up and opened on May 11, 2022. Public announcements were made about excavating the capsule. Curious and interested people were invited to watch the opening of the capsule and see its contents displayed to everyone. A little known secret is that the Public Works prepared the ground ahead of time to make the digging easy. When the work crew probed the ground to locate the time capsule, it had shifted away from where the granite time capsule marker sat on the park grounds. Once the site of the capsule was found, the workman dug down to the capsule and loosed the soil back up to the surface. Grass plots were put on top of the loosened soil to make the ceremonial digging look genuine. The Sesquicentennial Committee along with the 2021 Miss Tomato Fest, Ms. Maci Baker, had the honor of digging up the time capsule.

Committee members took turns loosening the soil

Recollections of Jacksonville

Cassie Devillier dug deep

Charlie Esco turned the soil

Sam Hopkins & Johnny Helm found it.

Before the big reveal, Mayor Randy Gorham welcomed the crowd to the much awaited occasion. Chairs were sat under the shady park trees on a day with pleasant weather for the 100 attendees.

The program began with pledges to the American and Texas flags. A hometown favorite country singer, CMA award winning singer Neal McCoy, led the singing of the national anthem.

After the program rituals and introductions, the capsule was carried to the display table for the opening the capsule. James Hubbard & Randy Gorham held the capsule as Randall Chandler sawed it open.

The time capsule contents were displayed on a table for all to see. After the event, the items were taken to the Vanishing Texanna Museum to be shown in a display case. All items became permanent possession of the museum for showings evermore.

Recollections of Jacksoville

A Message from Our Past and to Our Future

The capsule contained interesting contents. There were letters written to the mayor and city council, to the county judge, and to citizens from the Hackett family. Mayor Gorham read the letter from 1972 Mayor Phillip Pavletich to the 2022 city council. Pavletich made a comparison between 1962 prices and the costs in 1972. From the centennials' perspective, things had been getting a lot higher. However, Pavletich admitted that in 2022, we would view the 1972 costs as a bargain. The attending crowd laughed given the present 8.7% rate of inflationary prices. The inventory of the capsule included: a copy of the JHS newspaper, The Drumbeat, and copies of the Jacksonville Daily Progress; a phone book; a garter from a Jacksonville Belle; a KEBE radio recording of a centennial celebration; and several citations.

Mrs. Traci Wallace, one of the Sesquicentennial Committee members, arranged for her third class to watch a live video of the opening time capsule while in class at their school. The kids were excited about what they saw and were asked to remember it until 2072. Those children will be given the opportunity to write letters to their future selves, and have them placed in the bicentennial capsule. The class was invited to attend the burial of the capsule on December 10, 2022, and to come back to open it in 50 years.

Flag Day 2022

Flag Day Program June 14, 2022

Jacksonville has been observing Flag Day with a patriotic program on a regular basis for the last five years. Dr. Deborah Burkett has promoted and produced the local observance for the community to observe the national celebration. The program presentation was located in the Hazel Tilton city park near the War Memorial statue. American flags were flying in the breeze, filling the air with red, white and blue.

The flag was saluted and the national anthem was sung with passion and pride by Mrs. Phyllis Johnson, pictured with Dr. Deborah Burkett on the left.

Recollections of Jacksonville

During the program, Corporal Charles Broadway (deceased) was honored with an award in appreciation of his service in the Korean War with sentry dog Rex. The award was presented to his family by Mark Westbrook.

Dr. Burkett and Mayor Gorham with the Broadway family.

Other Veterans who were honored were the Dillehay Sisters of Jacksonville, Doris D. Jones and Hazel D. DuBose, World War II US Army Nursing Corps. The Flag Day committee is making a scrapbook of their military service and nursing careers.

PFC Robert Neal Scott was also recognized for his service during the Vietnam War where he was wounded in action on 26 November 1968. He was awarded the Purple Heart medal.

The award was presented to him by Chaplain Sam Hopkins. The program was closed by the song This Land Is Your Land performed by a combo band composing of Randy Gorham, Mike Kellogg, and the Lykins family.

Recollections of Jacksonville

Fred Douglas High School Centennial
July 30th, 2022

During the city sesquicentennial, the Fred Douglas Alumni Association, FDAA, held a reunion On Saturday, July 30, 2022 to celebrate the centennial of the opening of their high school in 1922. In those days the school was for segregated black children in Jacksonville. The high school graduated students until 1970, after which racial integration began. The purple and white dragons gathered in force. The morning began with a parade downtown. The crowd then proceeded to the former high school site that was across from the Lincoln City Park.

Recollections of Jacksonville

Old friends and their families met and embraced each other as they remembered good times back in the old days.

During the occasion a new school monument was unveiled as a perpetual memory of the old high school. The monument has an image of the Fred Douglas High School, images of the two school principals listing their tenures, the lyrics to the alma mater, and most importantly, the original 1951 dedication plaque from the old high school.

The purpose of the reunion was that future generations would remember the Fred Douglas High School. The school name has been continued as the title of the Fred Douglas Elementary School on Pine Street road. The young children at the reunion were encouraged to keep the memory alive from now on.

The Fred Douglas High School memorial also has a marker dedicated just to the former high school principals, M. B. Davis 1923-1956, and H. V. Jones 1956-1970. The pavilion has memorial bricks bought by FDAA members and others. The attendees spent time finding where the bricks they bought with their names on it were placed surrounding the marker.

One of the crowd pleasing activities was the burial of a time capsule. Elizabeth Whitaker was in charge of the event. People were allowed to bring items for the capsule, but it filled up before some of the crowd could add their items. Among the inclusions were several laminated letters from young children about what they want to be; letters and pictures from parents and grandparents; a copy of the FDAA proclamation; a flip phone with a charger, and a Blackberry phone with its charger; a commemorative pen; a centennial shirt; and a letter from the FDAA president to the future president with a report from the Fred Douglas Community Development Corporation to the future FDCDC members.

Historical Marker Dedication
September 21, 2022

Recollections of Jacksoville

Official Texas Historical Marker Dedication Ceremony for Jacksonville's Public Square Sept. 21, 2022 11AM to 12 Noon

Dedication at Hazel Tilton Park, E. Larissa and S. Main, Jacksonville

Presented by
Texas Historical Commission
Cherokee County Historical Commission
and Jacksonville's 150th Celebration Committee

The history of Gum Creek, the coming of the railroad, the founding of Jacksonville and its Public Square are all significant to Texas History. Happy Sesquicentennial!

- **Welcome** Randy Gorham, Mayor and Dr. Deborah Burkett, Emcee
- **Cherokee County Support for Historical Preservation** The Honorable Chris Davis, Cherokee County Judge
- **Pledges to the U.S. and Texas Flags** Elizabeth McCutcheon, Cherokee County Historical Commission (CCHC) Marker Program Chair
- **The Beginnings of Jacksonville** Keynote Speaker Texas State Senator Robert Nichols, District 3
- **Presentation of a Resolution Recognizing Jacksonville's Sesquicentennial** Senator Robert Nichols will present a copy to George Martin, Chair CCHC; to John Taylor, President of the Vanishing Texana Museum Board and to Sam Hopkins, Chair 150th Celebration Committee for the 2072 Time Capsule
- **Special Music** Mike Kellogg, First United Methodist Church, Jacksonville
- **Role of the Texas Historical Commission** Charles Sadnick, History Programs Division Director, Texas Historical Commission, Austin
- **Research for the Marker Application** Dr. Deborah Burkett, Cherokee County Historical Commission and Jacksonville's 150th Celebration Committee
- **Closing Remarks** James Hubbard, Jacksonville City Manager
- **Unveiling of the Marker** Texas Senator Robert Nichols, Texas Historical Commission Charles Sadnick, Cherokee County Judge Chris Davis, Mayor Randy Gorham, Dr. Deborah Burkett and program participants

Band Stand in Jacksonville's Public Square 1907

Early City Map by Mayor M. L. Earle 1914

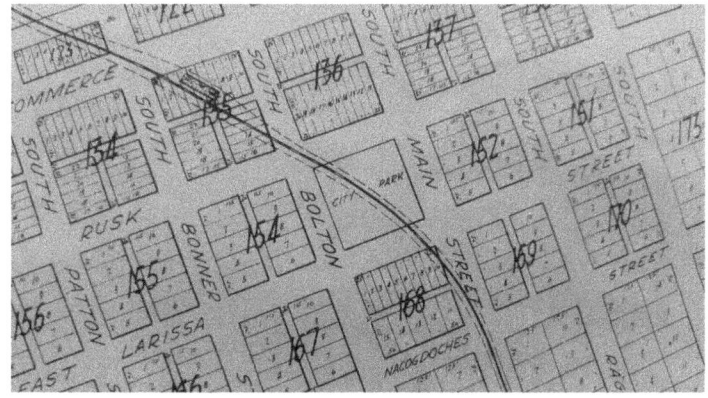

State Historical Marker: Jacksonville's Public Square Dedicated as part of the City Sesquicentennial Celebration
By Dr. Deborah Burkett

The following is but a small portion of the research submitted to THC in order to illustrate the significance of Jacksonville and its 150 years of history. Included in the application were many documents such as deeds, maps, letters, newspaper clippings, speeches and photographs. Topics covered included Gum Creek, the coming of the railroad in 1872, the establishment of "New" Jacksonville, the designation of a Public Square, schools, churches, business and commerce.

My thanks to all who helped with this project, especially to those who were kind enough to share memories of Jacksonville with me; their stories truly make history come alive. During these interviews I learned of doctors who treated employees of the railroad, of Mexican/Hispanic families whose ancestors worked for the railroad in the late 1800s and early 1900s. These stories add a dimension to the history of Jacksonville that had not been fully recorded to date.

In the Public Square, now known as Hazel Tilton Park, a Victorian-style band stand was built in 1907 and an early Jacksonville band would play concerts there. That band stand was replaced in the 1930s with one of native stone, a Works Progress Administration (WPA) project and bands continued to serenade citizens. Dr. Mary Alice Bone Adamson recalls, "…I remember in the summer there would be weekly concerts, old folks would be in their cars with the windows rolled down listening to the music…cars would be lined up, especially on Ragsdale Street…" This band stand was demolished in the 1960s to make room for a fire station."

"The Cotton Belt Railroad line would actually run through the Public Square. It came from Tyler and traveled to Lufkin, about ninety miles, running the full length of Cherokee County.

There were freight trains, especially when cars of tomatoes were shipped in early summer but it was the passenger service that affected most of the local people...The "Jitney" as it was called made stops at communities along the way such as Gresham, Flint, Bullard, Mount Selman, Jacksonville, Craft, Dialville, Rusk, Alto, Wildhurst, Forest and Wells."

Found in the late Minerva Bone Bassett's writings (Serendipitous Meandering) is the following personal memory, "...There were two Jitneys; one went from Tyler to Lufkin and back to Tyler and the other went from Lufkin to Tyler and back each day. The trains passed each other in Rusk. The Jitney consisted of two cars; the first was the gasoline/electric motor with a mail and freight section. The second car was for passengers. The Jitney didn't sound like a real train as it putt-putt-putted down the track. Its whistle was different too, so we never mistook the Jitney for a freight train. From the time I was about nine years old I rode the Jitney by myself. I would walk up to the station (in Jacksonville) and buy my 15 cent ticket from Mr. Aven for the twenty minute, eight mile ride to Mount Selman. I knew the route well. We passed Joe Wright High School and once out of town, we came to Hogan's Switch. This was a "Y" on the railroad where engines could turn around...soon we were crossing the long high trestle that crossed McKee's Gap. I was always nervous the Jitney would not stop long enough for me to get off. Once on the ground, I walked to my aunt's home."

Dr. Mary Alice Bone Adamson, youngest sister of Minerva, shares, "Our father, Dr. John Newton Bone, was the physician for employees of both the Missouri Pacific and Southern Pacific Railroads during the 1930s and 40s...as each had a train station here, we could ride on a

"pass" except for the Pullman (overnight sleeping car) which would cost us a fee, but it wasn't much! I looked through two of my father's ledger book which I've kept through the years. He rarely sent out a bill, so kept records of patient billing information in a ledger book so he could report the information for income tax purposes. I found in one of the books one page headed by these words: 'Southern Pacific Hospital – T&NO RR'. The page was dated 1953 and 48 names/charges were listed from January through December. A charge of $2.00 was listed by each name. A second column beside the first, has "by check" $2.00 – so I assume he was paid for the service done for each patient named by the SP with a check. I found the order for examination loose in the ledger at the site of the SP page. I copied it because it lists Morris S Fling as a "Carman Helper", so I assume this was one of the orders for an exam of a worker for the SP in 1955. I haven't found a page for the MP as yet, but it could have been in a lost ledger."

In a 1987 speech the late and longtime Chairman of the Cherokee County Historical Commission, John Allen Templeton II said, "...land was set aside specifically for a public park by the railroad officials...The park was located between my family home a few blocks from here on West Commerce Street and my Templeton grandparent's home which stood where the Central Baptist church's courtyard is today...As a child at play I spent many happy hours in the park, and as a member of the old Jacksonville City Band, which played concerts here every Friday night during the summers from that beautiful, Victorian bandstand built in the early 1900s..."

"The tracks were laid in the park in 1883. As early as the 1900's the city of Jacksonville was trying to get the railroad to remove itself out of the park. The tracks were placed there when the Kansas & Gulf Shortline Railroad (a narrow gage one) was being built from Tyler to Lufkin, backed by Tyler financiers. In 1887, it passed into the hands of the St. Louis, Arkansas and Texas Railway Company. On January 13, 1891, the property was sold to the Tyler Southeastern Railway Company. Eight years later it passed into the hands of the St. Louis Southwestern Railroad Company of Texas, popularly known as the Cotton Belt. Due to decreased patronage, the passenger service was discontinued in 1949."

M. L. Earle's Map of 1914 clearly shows the railroad route through the park. And the "ditch" that can be seen in the park provides physical evidence for us in 2022 that the railroad was there. Although the train no longer runs through the park, it still passes through Jacksonville. Now the train runs only in one direction. It comes from Palestine on its way to Longview.

Recollections of Jacksonville

The train no longer stops in Jacksonville or picks up passengers but does blow its horn at crossings and can be heard by fans sitting in the Tomato Bowl Stadium watching a Jacksonville High School football game or by diners eating at Sadler's Restaurant. The train and its sounds connect people to the past, a reminder of Jacksonville's beginnings.

Attendees readily absorbed and discussed the park's fascinating background.

State Senator Robert Nichols Speech at Dedication of Historical Marker

Recollections of Jacksoville

There have been 50 years from the Jacksonville Centennial in 1972 to the Sesquicentennial in 2022. A lot happened in those 50 years: the Vietnam War and two Gulf Wars; the invention of personal computers, the internet, smart phones, and great advances in medicine.

Now I want to take you back in time to the period here locally just before the founding of Jacksonville. In almost half the time I just covered, only 27 years before Jacksonville was founded in 1872, Texas became a State in 1845. At that time, Texas had not firmly established its borders. Even as a Republic, Mexico had not agreed that we were a Republic. We had not established counties along the Rio Grande River because of that. West Texas was not well established because the Comanche Indians controlled almost everything west of what is now I-35. There were no trains, and travel was by horse and wagon.

War between Mexico and the United States broke out and it was not until 1848 that our border was established. The treaty gave Texas parts of New Mexico, including Santa Fe, parts of Colorado, and up into Wyoming. Two years later, 1850, now only 22 years before our founding, the U.S. Congress finally adopted the current Texas boundaries.

Our first State Senator from Cherokee County was Joseph Hogg, father of Jim Hogg, later to become Texas Governor. To give you a feel of how rugged the old West was, just down the road in Rusk, State Senator Hogg set up an ambush of an attorney and newspaper man, on a Sunday morning, broad daylight, downtown Rusk. He waited between buildings and when the man came down the sidewalk, at pointblank range, he cut loose with both barrels of his double barrel shotgun and killed the man. He was never arrested.

From 1850-1870, Robert Guinn of Cherokee County served as State Senator. His family's descendants are still in our community. During that twenty-year period before Jacksonville was founded, the Civil War broke out and Texas seceded from the Union. After the war, in 1865, just 7 years before Jacksonville was founded, we went into a period of Reconstruction and were in a great recession. Carpet baggers came in and many people lost their land and businesses. During this period, the U.S. military, under force of arms, established a provincial government in Austin, changed our state constitution. Reconstruction did not end until 1876. There was a lot of corruption in the government in those days.

In 1869, our then County Judge, James Dillard, was elected to the Texas Senate in what was referred to as a "tumultuous" election. Cherokee County historians report that amid charges that ballot boxes were stolen, and that James Dillard had rightfully won, Cherokee County instead sent Myaman Priest to Austin, who was then declared ineligible by the Senate. After two more special elections, Dillard was finally seated in the Texas Senate. Dillard's opposition to Reconstruction won him enemies. He was twice expelled from the Senate for making speeches against bribery and corruption in the Legislature, but his constituency sent him back each time. One of the important bills he filed was to incorporate Jacksonville in SB 228.

Two years after Jacksonville was founded, in Austin, Senator James Dillard, with pistols in hand, along with two others, stormed into the Capitol, broke down the door of the corrupt Texas Governor Davis' office. They then removed state officials who refused to leave voluntarily. My Hero! Reconstruction ended four years after Jacksonville was founded in 1872 and a new constitution was written. As you can see, a lot happened just as Jacksonville was founded. The founders of Jacksonville, in spite of all the difficulties they had gone through with those tumultuous years, had an optimist vision for this city. They were right.

Recollections of Jacksoville

Walk Through History
October 16, 2022

Walk Through History
Jacksonville Old City Cemetery
October 16, 2022

Program: Historic Figures Speak

- **Frances Gaynelle Bailey Bone (b. 1895, d. 1944)** graduated from nursing school in 1919. During World War I and the flu epidemic, there was a need for more nurses. After receiving her RN, Gaynelle came to Jacksonville to work at the Cherokee Sanitarium which later became Nan Travis Hospital. (portrayed by Deborah Burkett)
- **M. L. Earle (b.1856, d.1932)** was elected mayor first in 1905 and served until 1911 and again from 1913 to 1919. Regarded as local historian; his 1914 map of Jacksonville still used today. Was Master of Ceremonies at the 1922 Jacksonville 50th Anniversary program in the City Park. (portrayed by Dr. John Ross)
- **Jackson Smith (b. 1814, d. 1897)** served in the Army of the Republic of Texas. As a Texas soldier, once stood guard over Santa Anna. At Gum Creek built a log house and blacksmith shop and served as the first postmaster. (portrayed by Andy Calcote)
- Special Music: Mike Kellogg and the Lykins Family

- **Odle Family (early settlers)** arrived at Gum Creek in a covered wagon. A member of the Odle family was reported by some to be the first burial in the Old City Cemetery. (portrayed by Antony Baker and Jamie Dorsey)
- **Melvina Chessher (b. 1833, d. 1940 at 106 and ½.)** This "Mother of Jacksonville" had five children and three husbands. Her son John believed to be the first boy born in "New" Jacksonville. She owned a hotel in downtown and became quite the celebrity. Her life heralded in publications throughout the state such as the Dallas Morning News. (portrayed by Nancy Nesselhauf)
- **Hiram and Amanda Spear (married in Cherokee County December 20, 1857)** Hiram served in the Confederacy at Fort Nelson, Arkansas, with the 18th Texas Infantry Company K. When Amanda heard of his illness she rode on horseback 300 miles through brutally cold weather to nurse him back to health. (portrayed by Shelley Cleaver and Betty Miller)
- **Alfredo R. Cavazoz (b. 1888, d. 1975)** Left Mexico and came to this country and to Jacksonville in 1928. He worked for the International and Great Northern Railroad for five years, then for the Cotton Belt railroad for twenty-five years. (portrayed by Roy Cavazoz Jr.)
- **Tribute to Honor all Veterans:** Prayer by Sam Hopkins

Preserving Our History at Old City Cemetery, Jacksonville

Cleaning Stones at Old City Cemetery

• Battle Hyman of the Republic by Mike Kellogg

• **Lula Seaton Hugghins** (b. 1900 in Oklahoma Indian Territory)
Her father died before she was born and family moved to Texas. As a teenager she went to work for C.W. and Adelia Puntch Nichols in their photography studio, first in the kitchen as a housekeeper and later in the studio. (portrayed by Barbara Hugghins)

• **John Martin** (b. 1877, d. 1970)
Soon I Will Be Done, sung a cappella by Phyllis Johnson African American reared in Alto. He and his wife moved to Jacksonville in 1910. He was self-employed, collected rubbish in the city. Later, John operated one of the first "service cars", as taxis were known at the time. (portrayed by George Martin)

• **Virginia Gray Mayfield** (b. 1923, d. 2013) graduated Fred Douglass High School. Attended Butler College in Tyler. Received Bachelor of Arts Degree from Jarvis Christian College in 1949. Taught Sunday School at Sweet Union Baptist Church in Jacksonville. (portrayed by Ginger Johnson)

• **Women Tomato Packers** by Kim Recognizing not only women who packed tomatoes but the families who built and operated the sheds, those who made the crates, baskets and the lugs. Names such as Braly, Armstrong, Mendoza, Long, Aber, Haberle, Box, Slover-Newton, Peacock and Dublin are just a few that come to mind.(portrayed Felt)

• **Eunice Sanborn** (b. 1895 or 96, d. 2011) in 2007, was listed in the Guinness Book of Records as the oldest living person in the world. Eunice and her second husband Wesley Garrett, along with C.J. Barbier, purchased nine acres of a peach orchard from John Wesley Love which became the site of the county's only cement lined Olympic size swimming pool (Love's Lookout) (portrayed by Janie Barber)
I'll Fly Away sung by crowd and led by Mike Kellogg and Lykins Family

Recollections of Jacksoville

History of Early Burials and Old City Cemetery

During the early settlement of the area, there were burials and cemeteries in many locations, but as years passed and land-owners changed, many have disappeared. Historians of the past wrote that the City Cemetery was used as a burial site for Anglo pioneers in the 1840s and some of the arrivals had migrated west with slaves. In 2022, no readable marked graves were found of anyone who might have lived and died in slavery. The City Cemetery was also referred to as Alexander Cemetery. The land on which the first cemetery was located consisted of five acres donated by Carnes Alexander and his father-in-law Frederick E. Becton. In the 1920's, old timers who were interviewed couldn't agree on who the first burial was. Among the first burials identified were: Samuel Odle, John Crunk, Miss Ellen Giffen, a man named Arrington, and a five year old granddaughter of Dr. Glidewell.

Out of Town Guests from Cedar Hill Cemetery in Rusk Viola Dickinson (b. 1881, d. 1971) studied piano at Juilliard in New York City and was a traveling piano teacher in the early 1900s.(portrayed by Betty Marcontell) **Sarah Summers (b. 1854, d. 1925)** Sarah's husband, James, was a businessman in Rusk. Together they lived in the beautiful Victorian house in downtown Rusk and raised five children. (portrayed by Joanne Hart)

Jacksonville Guest from Old City Cemetery: Minnie Pearl Lattimore Childs (b. 1884, d. 1974) mother of Margia Childs of Marja Brassiere Company. (portrayed by Patsy Lassiter).

On the Sunday for the Walk Through History, the weather was wet and rainy. There was the possibility that the costumed pageant might even have to be postponed. Dr. Deborah Burkett went ahead with the program because a tent had been set up to shelter up to 100 people. Miraculously, the rain stopped in time to start on time and take photos beforehand. Over 150 happy people saw and heard each historical person being portrayed by local impersonators. The performance drew such interest that it could easily performed again on future occasions for those who had stayed home due to the weather ahead of time.

Recollections of Jacksoville

Sesquicentennial Homecoming Celebration October 22nd, 2022

Sesquicentennial Homecoming Celebration Planning Committe

A highlight of the Jacksonville Sesquicentennial was the Homecoming Celebration downtown on Saturday, October 22, 2022. The weather was a perfect Fall day, with comfortable temperatures, and clear sunny skies. Kathleen Stanfill and Cassie Devillier planned, promoted, and produced a perfect event. The two ladies' executed the festivities so well that Sam Hopkins acclaimed them as being able to handle any operation, including the WW-II invasion of Normandy.

The promotion and publicizing of the downtown homecoming began with a huge banner draped on the side of a business building at the intersection of highways 69 and 79.

Recollections of Jacksoville

A pre-festival attraction was the pumpkin house that became a photo opportunity to create interest in the sesquicentennial homecoming day. The Fall flowers mixed with pumpkins beautified the lawn in the lot next to the Austin Bank. The decorations were the perfect background to our celebration.

On the Saturday festival day, A variety of entertaining activities were provided for the large crowd from 8:00 AM to 8:00 PM.

The day's schedule included:

8:00 AM – 4:00 PM	Artisans Market at the Postmasters Coffee Shop
9:00 AM	A prayerful gathering at 111 E. Commerce
10:00 AM	Community Choir at Tomato Bowl steps
10:30 AM	Patriotic kids bicycle parade
11:00 AM	Kids Activities throughout downtown
11:00 AM – 5:00 PM	Farmers market on Main Street
11:00 AM – 7:00 PM	Live music – Main at Commerce Streets
11:30 AM/1:30 PM/3:30 PM	Pumpkin Succulent Centerpiece Class
1:00 PM & 2:00 PM	Tomato Bowl tours
2:00 PM – 3:00 PM	Reminisce Room at Neighbors Coffee shop
2:00 PM – 5:00 PM	Collectible/Memorabilia Show Treasure Cove Mall
7:15 PM	Grand finale laser light show

Community Choir Concert

About 180 singers, half high school students and half adults, were under the direction of high school choir director Tiffany Hammock. They performed patriotic songs, a pop song, and a special number. composed by Hank Fellows entitled "One Heart, One Voice." Mr. Fellows flew from New York City to hear the community choir sing his song. Singers wore special shirt

Children's Bicycle Parade

Families from all over town brought their children with their bicycles to ride together in the kids' patriotic parade down Commerce Street.

Parade Begins!

Celebration on Commerce Street

The parade was preceded by a large American flag carried by a host of hardy volunteers. When the parade the onlookers continued to move westward on Commerce Street. Along the way they passed decorations on the street and on the buildings.

Recollections of Jacksoville

Among the many invited attractions was a reenactment group, the Texas Top Guns, who demonstrated a cowboy encampment.

Recollections of Jacksonville

Kids' activities were spread all around the festival grounds.

Young children flocked to them everywhere.

Parents marveled how much fun the brood could have for free.

There was even a petting zoo for those who like tame animals.

Food vendors were everywhere for the people who spent the day downtown.

Recollections of Jacksonville

The big attraction by far was the music stage. The opening act was the Plain Folks band with Mayor Randy Gorham playing the bass fiddle. There was plenty of picnic tables to enjoy the day and entertainment.
Local musician, singer, and recording artist, Johnny Helm had his group perform. Other musical acts were Michael Knight, Blindpursuit, Charles Denman and the East Texas Jazz Orchestra.

Committee member and event coordinator Kathleen Stanfill cruised around the festival to ensure all was going well.

Recollections of Jacksonville

The Jacksonville Sesquicentennial Celebration closed with the most sensation act ever brought to Jacksonville. Around 7:35 PM Saturday, October 22, 2022, a spectacular laser light show flashed on the big screen and then on the sides of buildings across from the music stage on Commerce Street. The amazed crowd loved the show and didn't want to go home after such a big show.

And so the festivities closed, creating many happy memories for those who attended it. This legacy has been recorded and placed in the bicentennial time capsule for future generations to enjoy. You really should have been there.

Each generation has the obligation to pass on the things they remember to those who will come after them. We are proud of Jacksonville and commend it to all who live here and will be here in the years to come.

May God bless you with freedom, prosperity, and much happiness.

Come back in 2072 and share the stories of your past, present and hopes for the future.

www.ingramcontent.com/pod-product-compliance
Lightning Source LLC
Chambersburg PA
CBHW062110290426
44110CB00023B/2767